I0500459

# Seeds of Old Wisdom:
# Proverbs from Many Countries

## Volume II of II

Available from Amazon.com and other fine retailers.

A production of:
Cedargrove
POB 244
Granby, CT  06035

ISBN-13: 978-1461082125

ISBN-10: 1461082129

Due to page size limitations, it was necessary to cut this into two volumes.  We would have preferred to do it as one volume.

# Table of Contents

## Dedication

I dedicate this book to:
- the family and community of the planet, and particularly
- my ancestors, who passed down their wisdom through proverbs and stories, and also
- my own family, especially my wife, wonderful daughters, and the unborn.

## Invocation

The ancient Greeks, and Romans, and many others, personified forces in the Universe. Those forces that inspire creative works were known as the Muses. Invocations to the muses sometimes began creative works of old. I have found them in books written in the 1800's. Perhaps they are merely a poetic convention, for some deep part of human consciousness. In that spirit, I invoke the Muses, and forces of wisdom, and the Deity and angels, in the name of humanity, to help humanity:

- commit random acts of beauty
- delight in truth, and awareness
- find its mission and purpose in life, and to embody it
- find wisdom
- know our Universe as light and information, and to delight in that
- learn respect, for from respect grows rapport, and communication, and cooperation, which is how humans survive
- learn the great power of words, and to use them wisely, for the good of all
- learn the often great power of kindness, and the often useless power of violence
- learn the power of attention, for what we concentrate on grows
- leave fear, and enter love
- leave folly
- realize their dreams, effortlessly, playfully, lovingly
- realize, that as the Navajo say, the purpose of life is the creation of sparkling, harmonious, joyful, healing beauty
- recognize that the search for truth is never ending
- recognize that we are all here to help each other
- see beauty in things apparently mundane
- take joy in small things, in family, and community

This is an old way to state intent. Let's sum my intent into a simple sentence: Joy for all. This book is my contribution to that end.

*Introduction*

Some would say that humans are unique because they use tools, and language. Animals use tools, and language, though. The one unique quality of humans is memory, extensive memory, with an ability to abstract. Animals do have memory, but not apparently as extensively as humans do.[1] Reintroducing animals where they've been hunted to extinction doesn't always work, because the herd memory, of where water, food, and shelter could be found, was eliminated. New herd memories have to be developed.

One reason it takes so long to raise a young human to competent maturity is that there is so much to learn. Humans survive by cooperation. Humans became humans in tribal groupings that cooperated. Language was an important part of that cooperation, and humanization. Human culture was oral for 99% of its existence. In an oral culture, wisdom must be compactly stored, and shared. The answer to this is proverbs, sayings, epigrams, maxims, and stories. Proverbs and stories are the crystallized wisdom of humanity.[2]

The book *Whispers of the Ancients: Native Tales for Teaching and Healing in Our Time*, by Tamarack Song, discusses this point, from the viewpoint of stories. Don Quixote at one point says to Sancho Panza that he is a soup of proverbs. I have found that many people enjoy hearing proverbs, and laugh at the funny ones, especially non-native speakers of English hearing them for the first time.

When I was studying Arabic, in college, I saw the professor write down words that students had difficulty with, on note cards. I asked why. He said he was assembling a dictionary- card by card. That is what I have done with this book. I've never seen so many proverbs in one place. One begins to see just how many, and how important, proverbs are to life.

*Deep truths are often so mundane they are invisible*. This applies to proverbs. In the time of William Shakespeare, people had trained memories, because books were rare and expensive. There were people who could listen to a 2 ½ hour play, and go home and write it out from memory. Fifty foreign languages were taught in Shakespeare's London, about 200 years before encyclopedias and dictionaries. How was that

---

[1] As an example, I was tracking a deer in the Pine Barrens of New Jersey. The deer was walking along, browsing, as shown by its tracks. It came upon a spent rifle cartridge on the ground. I could tell from the footprints that it immediately looked around, nervously, and bounded off at an angle. It clearly understood that danger was associated with this cartridge.

[2] The Wampanoag people say they live as long as their stories are told.

possible?   Trained memories, typically mnemonics.   Books were expensive in the USA until after WW II, and memory training was taught in school.   Nowadays, it is derided as rote learning.   When I took examinations, though, I found trained memory invaluable.

When I was studying languages, I memorized the basic text, which after the first few times took less time than studying the rest of the lesson.  I could do the exercises in class, without having looked at them, better than the students who had studied the lessons.   In addition, I retained the language much better, which meant less energy wasted on frustration.  I did better on examinations.. It was fascinating to read proverbs in foreign languages.  They grounded learning nicely.

Let us play with a metaphor.   Shark's teeth long outlast the shark. Consider cultural images.  We could consider the Roman imperial eagle. If you have a US quarter dollar coin, minted before about 2000, you see a Roman imperial eagle on the back.  This symbol has long outlasted the Roman state.  Metaphorically, it is like a shark's tooth- it cuts experience up into meaning.  Roman mythology, proverbs, and metaphors, are still very much a part of Western culture.

Proverbs, which are really very short stories, cut experience up into meaning.   They may be contradictory, just as experience can be contradictory.  The use of metaphor in proverbs is common.  The proverb *Little pitchers have big ears* does not refer to pitchers, it refers to the way children repeat what they hear, even if it is not something adults would want repeated.

Each culture crystallizes universal truth according to local metaphors. You will see this in any collection of proverbs.  Proverbs are refined if mundane bits of wisdom, often shared. They are tiny little stories, gems of wisdom that are easily shared.  One does not understand a culture until one knows the proverbs, and stories in it.  Proverbs and stories are the "software", the programming, of a culture.  One cannot understand Hindu culture without knowing something of Rama and Sita[3], for example.  In some areas of India, bride and groom dress as Sita and Rama, for the ceremony.

---

[3]   Who are themselves expressions of the archetypes of Vishnu and Lakshmi.

There is an Indian story about a student of a guru[4], who worked for years to be ready get his special mantra.  His teacher finally gave it to him- it was "Ram"[5], which is a very common name in India.

The student was upset- there was nothing special about Ram, so he left the teacher, and went to another.  The new teacher had the student shoveling manure all day long, for two years.  Finally, in desperation, the student asked the teacher for his special mantra.  The teacher said, "Ram".  The student said, "but that was what my last guru said, what's special about that?"  The new teacher said, "Yes, and you weren't ready to hear it before.  Are you ready to hear it now, or do you need to spend another year shoveling manure?"

Wisdom can be like this.  Proverbs, and stories, once understood, can keep us from that extra year of shoveling.  Will Rogers tells this story in a much shorter fashion, as a proverb- *a few people learn from books, a few from the mistakes of others, but the vast majority of humanity learns by peeing on the electric fence.* That proverb, and many others, are visceral.

Stories and proverbs leap cultures and language barriers.[6]  Three stories from the *Panchatantra* show up in Chaucer's *Canterbury Tales*, for example- or perhaps they came from a common source.  The *Tales of Uncle Remus* were traditional African teaching stories, reinterpreted in local metaphors.  As one example, the story of *Br'er Rabbit and the Tar Baby* is a powerful teaching story on the cycle of violence- Comparison, Resentment, Resistance, Revenge- which can run unconsciously in under one second.  The story brings the process into consciousness, using archetypal characters, so it can be halted.

Neville Goddard discussed metaphor in Biblical stories, which are an outgrowth of a much larger Semitic storytelling tradition, which also finds expression in Muslim, Sufi, and Rabbinical traditions.  I remember hearing, in an Anthropology class, about a story collected in the early 1800's, in Siberia, about a powerful shaman[7] who used to go to the Sun

---

[4]  Proverbs can be made from single words- Guru- *Gee, you are you-* a way of saying that a teacher helps you realize who you really are.

[5]  Ram is interchangeable with Rama, as Kuber is with Kubera, or Brahma with Brahm.

[6]  Idries Shah had a friend who was shocked to hear a beggar, in England, use the traditional request for alms, "Have ye any old iron", with the precise intonation used in the Shi'ite lamentation, "Ya Hasan, Ya Husayn".  Persians are fascinated with Shakespeare's name, which to them sounds like "Shaykh Pir", or "respected elder".  Dr. Glenn Norris notes that Northern Indian martial arts travelled northeast on the Silk Route, eventually becoming Ninjutsu, in Japan.  Ninjutsu is almost identical to Apache Wolverine martial arts.  Perhaps they came from a common source.  Idea transmission across traditional cultures, in the past, is fascinating.

[7]  The word Shaman is of Siberian origin, it refers to a spiritual master.  The Native American equivalent is sometimes called a Medicine man, or woman.

god, via the North pole, taking his sleigh- they use sleighs in Siberia- pulled by caribou, which are known as reindeer in Siberia because they can be harnessed to sleighs.

In the Arctic north, caribou are much more effective than horses, as draft animals. He would bring back presents and blessings for the people, on the sleigh. There is a lengthy tradition of shamans riding flying reindeer, in that part of the world, which goes back apparently more than millenia. Isn't it interesting that a story like this could cross cultural barriers to become an embedded part of American culture?

Similar proverbs show up across the Latin language spectrum. A Spaniard can understand spoken and written Italian, as an Italian can understand Spanish. Learning French comes easily to one raised speaking a Romance language. Some of these proverbs are also present in English, and have been apparently for centuries.

I read books of proverbs in Spanish. One can get a distinct image of what life might have been like, in a Spanish village. The mind thinks primarily in pictures, and images. Stories and proverbs are effective to the extent that they generate a clear image in the mind. Those who train animals note that if they make a picture in their minds, of what they want the animal to do, the animal will often do that. Those who fear animals may actually bring on what they fear. Let's have a proverb or two on this: *Energy flows where attention goes, and what you concentrate on grows,* followed by the Biblical *What you fear most will come upon you.*

Rudyard Kipling wrote a poem about an old schoolmaster who wrote a proverb on the chalkboard, each day. The proverbs were all he remembered of his schooling. I had a teacher who did this, when I was in high school. It was useful, and I remember the proverbs as well as I remember his description of how a Martin Mariner amphibious plane would pick up a pilot in a life raft, on the ocean, during WW II.

Forrest Gump cites the traditional proverb *Stupid is as Stupid does,* and a new one, *Life is like a box of chocolates, you never know what you're going to get.* Erma Bombeck titled one of her books based on the proverb *Life is a Bowl of Cherries,* asking why she got the pits. Jokes and proverbs can come in threes, which Georges Dumezil points out is a very Indo-European number.[8] Native Americans prefer four, and are very

---

[8]  American government, and the Christian image of God, have three parts. Consider triptych paintings.

puzzled by medicine which involves three doses, which seems to them incomplete.

My father had many proverbs, they were a part of everyday conversation. They were whispers of my ancestors.  I never realized how thoroughly Scots he was, in everything he did, until I started understanding Scottish culture.  Ethnic Scots in the USA don't seem to have a lot of ethnic memory, aside from proverbs.  It takes books like *Mark of the Scots*, and *Born Fighting,* to bring out what is unique among Scots.  *Cracker Culture* discusses survivals of Celtic culture, in the US.   Scots culture survives in proverbs.

After my father died, I collected all the proverbs he used to tell, as a sort of memorial, and added it to the others I had.  I realized how many there were, and began collecting more.  This book is the result.  I had hoped to have a comprehensive selection.  This book is comprehensive.  However, I do not believe I was able to collect even half the proverbs of my own native language, and fewer of the proverbs of my Celtic forebears. Except for those languages I know, I am limited in my choice of proverbs from other languages to translations, and sometimes these are already used in English, as English proverbs.  I found what I could.  I had to use the Sort function in Microsoft Word for this task.  This collection exceeds what Word will sort, I had to sort by sections.  The perfect is the enemy of the good.  I realized I could spend the rest of my life collecting proverbs, and not get even 10% of the total.  I have realized that this collection is at best a representative sample, a fraction, of the total universe of proverbs. I was originally only going to cite positive proverbs, leaving out, for example, proverbs about beating people with sticks.  But this distorts the whispers of the ancestors.  We recognize, but no longer use, these proverbs.

Many proverbs exhibit balance, or at least polarity, and a number were rhymed, or at least have meter.  *Little strokes fell great oaks* creates an immediate picture in one's mind.  The picture is immediately understood as a metaphor, on the value of focused small actions combining to eventually create a great effect.  It is far more effective than a longer prose presentation of the same idea.  Rhyme and meter make words much easier to remember- consider song lyrics- and often, traditional proverbs do rhyme.  Advertising jingles are a sort of perversion of rhymed proverbs.  They can be annoyingly persistent, especially since they have no wisdom in them.

My mother heard the 1930's Pepsi jingle *Pepsi, Pepsi, good for you...* on Thai television, in the late 1960s', and still remembered the English she heard as a child. As of this writing, I was unable to google it, but it lives on in my mother's memory. Some song lyrics may have a proverbial core.

Proverbs may have several characteristics.

1. Proverbs could be a direct statement of process, pattern, cause and effect, or polar balance, directly:

   *A man of words and not of deeds- is like a garden full of weeds*
   *He that laughs last laughs best*
   *Hope for the best and prepare for the worst*
   *One is never too old to learn*
   *Out of debt, out of danger*

2. Or metaphorical:
   [Standing on two stools] *Between two stools you fall to the ground*
   *A bird in the hand is worth two in the bush*
   *Still waters run deep*
   *Who repairs not his gutters repairs his whole house*

3. They may reflect an awareness of process and pattern, using parallel structure, that the young lack, as with the Arabic proverb, *Look for the mother [you* want to have for your children*], and marry her daughter,* or *seek the neighbor before you buy the house.* The last proverb also shows up on collections of Jewish proverbs, and I wouldn't be surprised to see Persian, Turkish, and even Oriental versions.

4. They may have several qualities:

   * They may reflect a positive view of life, as with *Forgive and forget.*
   * They may reflect a negative view of life, as with *Revenge is a dish that tastes best when it is cold.*
   * May rhyme, with a useful point, as with *All's well that ends well,* or be alliterative, as with *Proper Prior Planning Prevents Poor Performance.*

\* May seem extremely obvious, and be alliterative, as with *Practice makes perfect.*

\* May pithily note the wisdom of the least energy path, as with *First thrive and then wive,* which may make more sense for modern readers as be prosperous, then get married. The rhyme is easier to remember, though. I suppose one could say *be prosperous, then amorous,* to get the same idea across. The older form, though, like Biblical language, speaks to the subconscious mind.

\* May note the wisdom of years, in a shortened form easily passed on to those with little experience of life, as with *Honesty is the best policy.*

\* May offer wisdom in the form of humor, as with Woody Allen's *80% of success is showing up.* That is actually deep wisdom about the power of being present in the moment.

\* May veer into being maxims, as with Napoleon's *Order, Counter-Order, Disorder.*

\* May have a balance, as with *You get what you pay for, and you pay for what you get.*

\* May use parody to get a point across, as with *a gossip is one who has a sense of rumor.*

\* Proverbs based on parody may be particularly humorous. Take the standard proverb, *You can lead a horse to water, but you can't make him drink.* The parody is funny: *You can lead a kid to college, but you can't make him think.*

\* May reflect useful rules, such as *measure twice, cut once,* which in this case apply to at least carpentry and tailoring directly, and metaphorically to activities such as speeches.

\* Reflect the culture in which they were generated. *Always drink upstream from the herd* is a metaphor about not following the crowd, but it generates an immediate picture of cows at a river, drinking, and muddying the water, with a smart cowboy upstream, drinking.

5. Proverbs may communicate the same idea with different metaphors or statements.

- *A mill cannot grind with the water that is past*
- *Act without delay in an appropriate way*
- *Carpe Diem –Seize the Day*
- *Do all you can, where you are, with what you have, right now [Dr. Martin Luther King*

- *Make haste slowly*
- *Make hay while the sun shines*
- *Never put off till tomorrow what may be done today*
- *Now is all there ever was, is, or will be*
- *One today is worth ten tomorrows*
- *Opportunity seldom knocks twice*
- *Procrastination is the thief of time*
- *Some-a-day never comes -Some-a-day I'm a goin' to do this…*
- *Strike while the iron is hot*
- *Take time by the forelock*
- *There is danger in delay*
- *There is no time like the present*
- *Tomorrow never comes*
- *Water under the bridge comes not again to the mill*
- *What may be done at any time is done at no time*


6. Consider the following parallel, polar, and expanding structures:

- *80% of success is showing up -Woody Allen*
- *A contented mind is a perpetual feast*
- *A friend in need is a friend indeed.*
- *A good husband makes a good wife.*
- *A Jack of all trades is master of none.*
- *A rolling stone gathers no moss.*
- *Advice when most needed is least heeded.*
- *All work and no play makes Jack a dull boy.*
- *An ounce of discretion is worth a pound of wit.*
- *As you sow, so shall you reap.*
- *Barking dogs seldom bite.*
- *Better to ask the way than go astray*
- *Birds of a feather flock together.*
- *Children should be seen and not heard.*
- *Cut your coat according to your cloth.*
- *Desires are nourished by delays*
- *Discontent is the first step in progress*
- *Don't put all your eggs in one basket*
- *Everybody's business is nobody's business.*
- *Example is better than precept.*
- *First come, first served.*
- *Footprints on the sands of time are not made by sitting down.*

- *Good company on the road is the shortest cut*
- *Great oaks from little acorns grow.*
- *Happy is the country that has no history*
- *He that would the daughter win, must with the mother first begin.*
- *Health is wealth*
- *Idle folk have the least leisure*
- *It is better to give than to take.*
- *It is easy to be wise after the event.*
- *Know your own faults before blaming others for theirs.*
- *Knowledge is power.*
- *Lend your money and lose your friend*
- *Look before you leap*
- *Love your neighbor, yet put not down your fence*
- *Make hay while the sun shines.*
- *Man proposes, God disposes*
- *Many hands make light work.*
- *Many kiss the hand they wish to cut off.*
- *Many would be cowards if they had courage enough*
- *Marry in haste, repent in leisure*
- *Necessity is the mother of invention.*
- *Never spend your money before you have it.*
- *Nothing ventured, nothing gained*
- *Of circumstance, complain not much For the Lotus grows in muck[9]*
- *One good turn deserves another.*
- *Only the wearer knows where the shoe pinches.*
- *Praise without profit puts little in the pot.*
- *Prosperity makes friends, adversity tries them.*
- *Self-praise is no recommendation*
- *Success has many friends.*
- *The darkest hour is that before dawn[10]*
- *The early bird catches the worm.*
- *The proof of the pudding is in the eating.*
- *The tongue ever turns to the aching tooth.*
- *Things may come to those who wait, but only the things left over by those who hustle.*
- *Through obedience, learn to command.*
- *Uneasy lies the head that wears a crown*

[9] A Chinese proverb- which means that a thing of great beauty can grow in what appear to be bad circumstances.
[10] This is very Chinese, also, and reflects an awareness of polarity.

11. Proverbs easily cross linguistic barriers, just as stories do. *He gives twice who gives quickly* is an English rendering of the Latin *Bis dat qui cito dat* .   The following Latin proverbs are still known, in Latin:

- *Caveat emptor, Let the buyer beware.*
- *In vino veritas, In wine, there is truth.*

One finds French proverbs: *Cherchez la femme*  [Look for the woman][11]

12.  Proverbs may offer seemingly contradictory pieces of advice, as with *Absence makes the heart grow fonder* vs. *Out of sight, out of mind.*

13.  There are even proverbs specific to a certain field.  Consider these proverbs about health:

- A good surgeon must have an eagle's eye, a lion's heart, and a lady's hand
- A sound mind in a sound body
- *After dinner sit a while, after supper walk a mile*
- Alkalinize or die
- All disease is the result of blockage -Yellow Emperor's *book of Internal Medicine*
- All medicine is food, and all food is medicine.  Some kinds work better than others.
- *An apple a day keeps the doctor away*
- An old doctor, a young lawyer, [an old carpenter, a young sawyer]
- Better lose a supper than gain a hundred physicians
- Better no doctor at all than three -Polish
- Bitter pills may have blessed effects
- Butter is gold in the morning, silver at noon, lead at night
- Cider on beer, never fear; beer upon cider, makes a bad rider
- *Dark bread makes cheeks red, white bread makes people dead* -German
- Death is in the pot -Dutch
- Death is the poor man's best physician -Irish
- Desperate diseases must have desperate cures

---

[11]   In murder mysteries, for example, or in political scandals, look for the woman, to find the origin. An American equivalent is *Follow the money,* or *Who benefits from this?* One notices from proverbs that different cultures have a different focus.

- Diet cures more than the doctor.
- Diet cures more than the lancet -Hindustani
- *Disease is soon shaken By physic soon taken* -English
- Disease of the soul are more dangerous than those of the body.
- Disease, enemy, and debt --these three must be cut off as soon as they begin to fester.
- Diseases are the interest of pleasures -English
- Diseases are the price of ill pleasures.
- Diseases come on horseback, but go away on foot
- *Diseases of the body, and diseases of the mind  in the tongue the doctor and philosopher find*
- Doctor's faults are covered with earth, and rich men's with money.
- Doctors are men who prescribe medicines of which they know little, to cure diseases of which they know less, in human beings of whom they know nothing -Voltaire [Francois-Marie Arouet]
- *Doctors errors are erased, by soil with shovel well emplaced*
- Doctors make the very worst patients
- Don't dig your grave with your own knife and fork -English
- Don't treat the symptom, instead find the cause.
- Easier to stay well than to get well.
- *Eat meals slowly, and not much-that you may a century touch.*
- Eat to live and not live to eat
- *Eat well, drink in moderation, and sleep sound, in these three good health abound* -Latin
- Every disease will have its course
- Exercise, temperance, fresh air, and needful rest are the best of all physicians
- Feed a cold, starve a fever
- *Feed by measure, long life's pleasure.*
- Feed sparingly and defy the physician.
- *Fond of lawsuits, little wealth  fond of doctors, little health.*
- Fresh pork and new wine- kill a man before his time.
- Glutton: one who digs his grave with his teeth -French
- Gluttony has killed more than the sword -French, Italian
- Go not with every ailment to the doctor, nor with every plaint to lawyer -Portuguese
- God heals and the doctor takes the fee - Benjamin Franklin
- Graves are dug with a spoon
- Health is better than wealth

- If doctors fail thee, be these three thy doctors; rest, cheerfulness, and moderate diet.
- *If simple herbs suffice to cure, 'tis vain to compound drugs endure.*
- If the doctor cures, the sun sees it; but if he kills, the earth hides it -Russian
- If the patient dies, the doctor has killed him, but if he gets well, the saints have saved him -Italian
- If the pills were pleasant, they would not be gilded.
- If you don't want to be sued, love your patients -Bernie Siegel
- If you have a friend who is a physician, send him to your enemy's house -Portuguese
- Laugh at your ills, And save doctors' bills.
- Laughter is the best medicine.
- Like cures like.
- Many dishes make many diseases.
- Medicine can prolong life, but death will seize the doctor, too.
- Medicine is the art of guessing -Latin
- Medicine left in the container can't help - Yoruba
- Medicines are not meant to live on.
- Men dig their graves with their teeth -Dutch
- Nature, time, and patience are three great physicians.
- Never go to a doctor whose office plants have died -Erma Bombeck
- No good doctor ever takes physic -Italian
- No physician like a true friend -Rumanian
- One doctor makes work for another
- One hour's sleep before midnight is worth two hours after
- *Past cure, past care.*
- Patience is a plaster for all sores.
- Patience is poultice for all wounds -Irish
- Patience is the best medicine.
- Patience is the best remedy.
- Patience is the cure for all suffering -Latin
- Peace is the best medicine -Latin
- Physician, heal thyself! -Latin
- Physicians rarely take medicine -Danish
- Physicians' faults are covered with earth -Rumanian
- Rich food, rich coffin
- Said the wealthy man, "Doctor, strike at the root of the disease",

and smash went the decanter under the faithful physician's cane.
- Sickness soaks the purse.
- Sometimes the remedy is worse than the disease -Francis Bacon
- Study sickness while you are well; before you thirst, dig your well.
- The best doctor knows the worthlessness of the most medicines -Benjamin Franklin
- The best physicians are Dr. Diet, Dr. Quiet, and Dr. Merryman
- The disease built from the bowl will not be easily healed by a pill
- The beginning of health is sleep -Irish
- The doctor amuses the patient while nature does its work -Voltaire
- The doctor is often more to be feared than the disease -French
- The doctor must heal his own bald head -Persian
- The doctor seldom takes physic -Italian
- The first step to health is to know that we are sick.
- *The grave may be dug very soon- with a knife, and fork, and spoon.*
- The operation was a success, but the patient died.
- The patient is not likely to recover who makes the doctor his heir -Thomas Fuller
- The remedy oft kills more than the disease.
- The smaller the waistline, the longer the life.
- There are no incurable diseases, only incurable patients.
- *Those of health and lengthy life avoid the Doctor's pills and knife.*
- *Those who would last, must sometimes fast*
- You become what you eat

14. I had originally thought I could collect the great majority of proverbs. After collecting what you see here, I realized that I had less than a majority of the world's proverbs. There are many more than I can list. Let's see what proverbs say about proverbs:

- A country can be judged by the quality of its proverbs -German
- A proverb is one man's wit and all men's wisdom - Lord John Russell
- A proverb is the child of experience -English
- A proverb often flashes light on regions where reason shines but dimly -Martial
- A proverb is a story in a sentence.
- A proverb tells the truth -Polish
- Advice after injury is like medicine after death - Danish

- Epigrams succeed where epics fail -Persian
- *He misses what is meant by epigram  who thinks it only frivolous flim-flam*
- He who tells the stories rules the world -Hopi
- Hold fast to the words [proverbs] of your ancestors - Maori
- Hold fast to the words of your ancestors -Hopi
- Patch grief with proverbs.
- Proverbs are short sentences drawn from long experience.
- Proverbs are the children of experience -English, Sierra Leone
- Proverbs are the cream of a nation's thought.
- Proverbs are the daughters of daily experience -Dutch
- Proverbs are the lamp of speech.
- Proverbs are the palm oil with which words are eaten - Nigerian
- Proverbs are the wisdom of the ages.
- Proverbs are what remains, when education is forgotten.
- Proverbs bear age, and he who would do well may view himself in them as in a looking glass -Italian
- The wisdom of nations lies in their proverbs, which are brief and pithy.
- *Three things must epigrams, like bees, have all- a sting, and honey, and a body small* -Latin
- What is an epigram? *A dwarfish whole, its body brevity and wit its soul* –Coleridge
- When education is forgotten, proverbs are what remain.
- Wise men make proverbs, but fools repeat them without thinking - Samuel Palmer

Since we are discussing health, there are other points of traditional culture, which exist without a lot of awareness of their value, just like proverbs. Lemonade was originally an alkalinizing drink, very useful to maintain health. Roman soldiers mixed old-fashioned vinegar in their water, for the same reason. People in the West Indies take lemon juice with seafood, to avoid allergic reactions. Ginger Ale, and Root Beer, were spring tonics, designed to clean the body of the toxins built up during winter. When after dinner mints were made of mint, the herb, they were very helpful to digestion. These things have been cheapened, but they are easily revived. Traditional spas, which took people from very hot water to very cold water, and back, improved circulation, and toxin removal, greatly. They were very effective. They were largely abandoned in the 1800's only due to Victorian ideas about nudity.

There are three major sensory systems- visual, auditory, and kinesthetic. Persons who prefer the visual modality tend to speak very rapidly, because their minds work in flashing pictures which move quickly. Auditory persons speak more slowly, because they hear voices. Kinesthetic people speak very slowly, because they work from feeling. Athletes sometimes come across as "slow", due to their kinesthetic orientation.  American culture has gone from auditory to visual, and it moves faster and faster.  This is not the best state to be in, all the time. Slip into the auditory modality- slow down, enjoy wisdom.  The rest will do you good.  In Bangla Desh, and some Arab countries, poets can be as popular as rock musicians, because people still appreciate the beauty of words.  What would country music be, without words?  It is the direct descendent of Irish and Scots ballads.

15. New proverbs are very interesting.  Consider *When the pin is pulled, Mr. Grenade is not our friend*, or *The only time a plane has too much fuel is when it is on fire*.  These date to the 20<sup>th</sup> century, yet they are proverbs.

A collection of proverbs, of this size, could be made from most languages. It took me twelve years to gather these, and it is as if I had only started. Plato said *the perfect is the enemy of the good,* so I decided to make this available.  It is difficult to say where a proverb originated.  As I read this, I realized that Ben Franklin apparently had access to Romance language proverbs- or English had already picked them up in his time.  This collection is already so long that my Wordprocessing program's Search function doesn't work, and the Sort function can only be used on sections of the book.

I took what I could find, for source, but often cannot vouch for the source. Since these proverbs are now all available in English, perhaps source doesn't matter so much.  Also, a number of proverbs have equivalents in English.  This makes translation difficult- a literal translation does not give as accurate a meaning as the equivalent English proverb.  Perhaps proverbs are like people- where they came from doesn't matter so much as who they are.

As you start looking at this collection, here's a thought to guide you:

*Small minds speak of little things*
*lesser minds of other people*
*Habit of your spirit sings*
*Religion crystallizes under steeple*
*Great minds seek out great ideas*
*Wisdom soon awareness seizes*

*Seek the essence, not the stuff*
*and you'll have more than enough*
*We control but our intention*
*from that, for us, doth flow creation*
*Mountaintop is good for some*
*in bliss, I'd rather have some fun*
*This, the most important thing*
*feel good, allow your heart to sing*

*Quackery has no friend like credulity*
Quality is better than quantity
Quality matters more than quantity
Quality, not quantity
Quarreling dogs come halting home
Quarrelling is the weapon of fools
Quarrels end, but words once spoken never die
*Quarrels never could last long, if on one side only lay the wrong* -Ben Franklin
Quarrels of lovers but renew their love
Quarrels take two, and both are to blame
Quarrels would not last long if the fault was only on one side -Rochefoucauld
Quarrels, like fires, are easily begun, but with difficulty put out
Quick and well don't agree -Italian
Quick and well seldom go together -Danish
Quick at meal, quick at work
*Quick believers need broad shoulders*
Quick feet and busy hands fill the mouth
Quick giving is the best charity
*Quick stitches save the britches*
Quickly come, quickly go
Quiet is a great treasure
Quiet people are well able to look after themselves -Irish
Quietness is best
Quietude is the crown of life
Quit griping about your church; if it was perfect, you couldn't belong
Quit while you're ahead
Quite often you can prove your command of the language by saying nothing
*Radiant smile and happy woman, comes of husband's loving acumen -Spanish*
Rage avails less than courage -French
Rage is without reason
*Rags to riches to rags* -Lancastrian
Rain beats a leopard's skin, but it does not wash off the spots -Ashanti
*Rain before seven; clear/fine before/by eleven* -English
Rain comes oft after sunshine, and after a dark cloud a clear sky -Danish
Rain does not fall on one roof alone -Cameroonian
Rain wets a leopard's skin, but it does not wash out the spots -Twi [Ghana]
Raise not crows that would tear out your eyes -Spanish
*Raising children can be simple- education, love, and good example*

Rarely are there fish under a willow tree - Japanese
*Rather a bit correctly than much incorrectly* -Norwegian
Rather a husband with one eye than with one son -Portuguese
*Rather a single grape for me than a brace of figs for thee* -French
Rather an ass that carries than a horse that throws -Italian
Rather free in a foreign place than a slave back home -Norwegian
Rather go rob with good men than pray with bad -Portuguese
*Rather go to bed supperless than run in debt for a breakfast* - Ben
Franklin
Rather hat in hand than hand in purse -Italian
Rather have a little one for your friend, than a great one for your enemy
-Italian
Rather lose the wool than the sheep -Portuguese
Rather the egg to-day than the hen to-morrow -Danish
Rats and conquerors must expect no mercy in misfortune -Danish
Rats leave/desert/forsake a sinking ship
*Rats make havoc in the kitchen when the cat's a mewling kitten*
Ravens do not peck out raven's eyes -Italian
Raw cucumber makes the churchyards prosperous -English
Raw leather will stretch -English
Read much, but not too many books -Ben Franklin
Read not books alone, but men
Readiness is all
Reading enriches the mind
Reading is to the mind what exercise is to the body
Reading makes a full man, meditation a profound man, discourse a clear
man
Reading maketh a full man, conference a ready man, and writing an exact
man
Ready money is ready medicine
Ready money works great cures -French
Real heart lied never
Realism...has no more to do with reality than anything else -Hob Broun
Really to stop criticism one must die -French
Reap as/what one has sown
Rear sons for help in old age; and store up grains against famine
Reason answers questions, imagination asks them
Reason binds the man
Reason deceives us often, conscience never
Reason explains the darkness, but it is not a light- Noah benShea, *Jacob
the Baker*
Reason governs the wise man, a cudgel, the fool
Reason is the guide and light of life

Reason lies between bridle and spur -Italian
*Reason not with the great, 'tis a perilous gate* -French
Reason rules all things
*Reason's whole pleasure, all the Joys of Sense Lie in 3 words: health, peace, and competence  but health consists in temperance alone, and Peace, O Virtue! Peace is all thine own*
Reasonable people can differ -French
Reasonings banish reason -French
Rebuke is greater to the wise than hundred blows on a fool -Ghana
Rebuke with soft words, and hard arguments
Rebukes ought not to have a grain more of salt than of sugar -French
Receive as you give
Receive gifts with a sigh, for most men give to be paid -Irish
Reckless youth makes rueful age -French
Recognize that alternatives exist but make sure they all bear on the object
Reconciled friendship is a wound ill salved -Italian
Reconciled friendship is like a badly healed wound -Danish
Record only the sunny hours
*Red sky at night, shepherd's/sailor's delight; red sky in the morning, shepherds/sailors take warning*
Reflection insures safety, but rashness is followed by regrets
Reforms are most unpopular where most needed
Refraining from all evil, not clinging to birth and death, working in deep compassion for all sentinent beings, respecting those over you and pitying those below you, without any detesting or desiring, worrying or lamentation - this is what is called Buddha. Do not search beyond it -Dogen
Refuse a wife with one fault, and take one with two -Romanian
Refusing to ask for help when you need it is refusing someone the chance to be helpful
Regardless of what happens, somebody always claims he knew it would
Rehab is for quitters!
*Rejoice in little, shun what is extreme; the ship rides safest in a little stream* -Dutch
Relatives are friends from bitter necessity
Relatives are the worst friends, said the fox as the dogs took after him -Danish
Religion is the best armor, but the worst cloak
Religious contention is the devil's harvest -French
Remember as far as anyone knows, we're a nice normal family -Homer Simpson
Remember that everyone you meet is afraid of something, loves

Seeds of Old

Riches br(
Riches bri
Riches do
Riches eit
Riches ha
Riches rur
Riches se
Rid the wo
Ride on, b
Ridicule is
Right can
Right or w
Rise early
Rise early
Assiniboin
Risk is pai
Acquisitior
Risk more
Dream mc
is possible
Rituals mu
Rivalry of :
Rivers nee
Roast gee
Roast pige
Roasted p
Rocks nee
Roll my loç
Roll seven
Roll with th
Rome is nc
Rome was
Rooster to
Roosters' t
Rosary in I
Roses fall,
Rudeness
Rudeness
Rule 172 (
Acquisition
Rule 177 K
Rule of Ac(
Rule youth

something, and has lost something -French
Remember that great love and great achievements involve great risk or great awareness and great change
Remember that not getting what you want is sometimes a wonderful stroke of luck -Dalai Lama
Remember that silence is sometimes the best answer -Country wisdom
Remember that time is money - Ben Franklin
Remember that where you go hereafter may depend on what you do after here
Remember that your children are not your own, but lent to you by the Creator  –Mohawk
Remember the three R's: Respect for self; Respect for others; and responsibility for all your actions
Remember thou art but a man
Remember, today is the tomorrow you worried about yesterday - Dale Carnegie
Remove emotion, and pure reason returns, which brings intuition, and understanding and peace -Mexican
Remove the weeds by the root, or they grow again next Spring -Chinese
Render unto Caesar the things that are Caesar's
*Repair your roof when shines the Sun, or you'll wish this thing you'd done*
Repay evil with kindness
Repeating is the mother of learning -Latin
Repentance comes too late -Polish
Repentance costs dear -Spanish
Repentance costs very dear -French
Repentance is good, but innocence is better
Repentance is the heart's medicine
*Repetition is the mother of knowledge/erudition*
Repetition is the mother of study -Latin
*Repression is the seed of revolution*
Reprove thy friend privately, and commend him publicly
Republicans will do anything for the poor except get off their backs
Reputation helps you get a job. Character helps you keep it.
Reputation is often got without merit and lost without fault
Reputation is what people think you are. Character is what you are.
Reputation is what you are in the light, and character what you are in the dark.
Repute hangs a man -French
Resentment is like taking poison and hoping the other person dies  –St. Augustine
Resist in the beginning; too late is the medicine prepared when evil has grown strong for a long time -Ovidius

| | |
|---|---|
| *Resist wit* | Rules are made to be broken |
| Resolute | Rumour grows as it goes |
| Resolve t( | Rumour has wings -Vergilius |
| Respect a | Rumour is not always in error, sometimes it chooses -Tacitus |
| Respect a | Run/Hold with the hare and hunt/run with the hounds |
| *Respect i* | Run as hard as a wild beast if you will, but you won't get any reward |
| Respect is | greater than that destined for you -Egyptian |
| rapport, a | Runnin' away from problems is a way to run right into them -Country |
| how huma | wisdom |
| Respect tl | Running water carries no poison -Italian |
| Respect tl | Rush slowly |
| Respect y | Russian wolves live by using their own legs -Russian |
| Responsit | Rust consumes iron, and envy consumes itself -Danish |
| Rest bree( | Rust eats up iron |
| Rest is go | Rust wastes more than use -French |
| Rest is sw | *Sables feel proud in the absence of ermine* |
| Rest make | Sacrificing means more |
| Rest witho | Sadness and gladness succeed each other -French |
| Return to ( | Sadness is but a wall between two gardens -Kahlil Gibran |
| there to m( | Said the wealthy man, "Doctor, strike at the root of the disease", and |
| Return wh( | smash went the decanter under the faithful physician's cane |
| Revenge a | Sail beyond sight of the shore would you discover new land |
| Revenge c | Sail while the breeze blows, wind and tide wait for no man -Danish |
| Revenge i | Sail while the wind blows; wind and tide wait for no man |
| Revenge i | Saint cannot if God will not -French |
| Revenge i | Saintliness is also a temptation -Jean Anouilh |
| Reverence | Saints appear to fools -Portuguese |
| Revolution | Saints don't fill the belly -Portuguese |
| Revolution | Saints fly only in the eyes of their disciples -Hindi |
| Revolution: | Salt seasons all things |
| Reward an | Salt water and absence wash away love |
| -Ferengi R | Sarcasm poisons reproof |
| Reward be | Satan always finds work for idle hands |
| Reward sw | Satisfaction is not guaranteed -Ferengi Rule of Acquisition |
| Reynard [tl | Sauce for the goose is sauce for the gander -English |
| Rice eaten | Save a stranger from the sea, and he'll turn your enemy |
| Rich folk ha | Save a thief from gallows and he will help hang you |
| Rich food, | Save a thief from the gallows and he will hate you |
| Rich garme | Save a thief from the gallows and he'll be the first who shall cut your |
| Rich man n | throat -Italian |
| Rich men k | Save for a rainy day - Aesop |
| Riches and | Save money and money will save you -Jamaican |
| *Riches are* | Save something for the man that rides on the white horse -Italian |

Save us from our friends -Italian
*Save while you may, no morning sun lasts a whole day*
*Save your breath to cool your broth* -Portuguese
Saving is getting -French
Saving mustard seeds in hand, while a watermelon escapes -Kashmiri
Savings are the first gain -Italian
Say "bless you" when you hear someone sneeze
Say but little and say it well -Gaelic
Say it tomorrow if you have something to say -Japanese
Say no ill of the year till it be past
Say not all that you know, believe not all that you hear
Say nothing but good about the dead -Horatius
Say well is good, but do well is better,
Say what we will, do what we will, the boat goes but sorrily without oars
-Italian
Saying "sweets" won't make your mouth sweet -Azerbaijani
Saying and doing are two things -Italian
Saying is one thing, doing another -Italian
Saying well causes a laugh; doing well produces silence -French
Scabbed horse cannot abide the comb
Scald not your lips in another man's pottage
*Scant feeding of man or horse, is small profit and sure loss*
Scatter with one hand, gather with two -Slavic, Welsh
Scattering is easier than gathering -Irish
Scholar's ink lasts longer than martyr's blood -Irish
Science has no enemy[ies] but the ignorant
Science is organized knowledge. Wisdom is organized life -Immanuel Kant
Science may never come up with a better office communications system than the coffee break
Score twice before you cut once
Scornful dogs will eat dirty puddings
Scratch a Russian, and you find a Tartar
Scratch me and I'll scratch you
Scratch my back and I'll scratch yours -American
Scratch people where they itch -French
Scratch where it itches
Search others for their virtues, thyself for thy vices - Ben Franklin
Seat yourself in your place, and they in theirs
Second thoughts are best -Italian
Secrecy is the beginning of tyranny -Italian
Secrecy is the enemy of efficiency, but don't let anyone know it
Secrecy is the soul of all great designs

Secret gifts are openly rewarded -Danish
*See a pin and let it lie, you'll want a pin before you die* -French
*See a pin and pick it up, all the day you'll have good luck; see a pin and let it lay, bad luck you'll have all day* -French
*See how the boy is with his sister and you know how the man will be with your daughter*-Lakota
See life through an artist's eye
See Naples and then die -Italian
See no evil, hear no evil, speak no evil -Italian
See that your own hearth is swept before you lift your neighbor's ashes -Gaelic
See the big picture without judgment, and understand it immediately -Japanese
See with your mind, hear with your heart -Kurdish
See your sons and daughters: they are your future  —Oneida
See, listen, and be silent, and you will live in peace
*Seeds sprout, and the truth will out*
*Seeing is believing* -Italian
Seeing is better than hearing
Seeing is different than being told
Seeing much, suffering much, and studying much are the three pillars of learning
Seek advice but use your own common sense -Yiddish
Seek and ye shall find
Seek counsel of him who makes you weep, and not of him who makes you laugh -Arabic
Seek first the neighbor, then the house -Arabic, Jewish
*Seek home for rest, for home is best*
Seek not the truth, only cease to cherish opinions -Zen
Seek out first the woman you'd be married to in 20 years, and marry her daughter -Arabic
Seek out the mother you want for your children, and marry her daughter -Arabic
*Seek the essence, not the stuff- and you'll have more than enough*
Seek the truth from facts
Seek the ways of the eagle, not the wren -Omaha
Seek truth in meditation, not in moldy books. Look in the sky to find the moon, not in the pond -Persian
*Seek virtue and of that possessed, to Providence resign the rest* - Ben Franklin
Seek wisdom, not knowledge.  Knowledge is of the past, wisdom is of the future. —Lumbee
Seize/Take time by the forelock

Seize on opportunity - but not any opportunity
Seize opportunity by the beard, for it is bald behind -Bulgarian
Seize the day  [Carpe diem] -Horace
Seldom seen, soon forgotten -Italian
*Seldom spurred the better horse, let it gently run the course*
Select, don't settle
Self conceit may lead to self destruction -Aesop
Self do, self have
*Self worth, service to others; they are close like brothers*
Self exaltation is the fool's paradise -Italian
Self praise is half slander
Self praise is no recommendation - Romanian
Self praise stinks
Self-confidence is essential to great undertakings
Self-confidence is the first requisite to human greatness
Self-control is courage under another form
Self-distrust is the cause of most of our failures
Self-help is the best help -Aesop
Self-love is blind -Dutch
Self-love nobody else's love -Dutch
Self-praise is no praise at all -English
Self-praise is no recommendation
Self-preservation is the first law of nature
Self-reverence, self-knowledge, self-control, these three alone lead life to sovereign power
Self-trust is the essence of heroism
Self-trust is the first secret of success
*Sell me dear, and measure me fair* -Italian
Sell not honey to one who keeps hives -Portuguese
Sell not the bear's skin before you have caught him -Italian
Sell not virtue to purchase wealth, nor liberty to purchase power - Ben Franklin
Sell the sizzle, not the steak -Ferengi Rule of Acquisition
Send a boy where he wants to go and you see his best pace
Send a man of sense on the embassy, and you need not instruct him -Portuguese
Send a thief to catch a thief
Send a wise man on an errand, and say nothing to him
Separation secures manifest friendship - Indian
*September blow soft till the fruit's in the loft* - Indian
Serenity is not freedom from the storm, but calmness within the storm
Serve a lord, and you will know what it is to be vexed -Portuguese
Serve as a serf, or fly like a deer -French

Serve somebody with the same sauce
Serve the masses, dine with the rich; serve the rich, dine with the masses
Service is greatness -Kashmiri
Service is not inheritance -Italian
Service with resentment is no service
Set a beggar on horseback, and he'll ride to the devil
Set a beggar on horseback, and he don't trot, but gallops -Dutch
Set a beggar on horseback, and he 'll out ride the Devil -German
Set a fool to roast eggs, and a wise man to eat them
Set a fox to catch a fox -Danish
Set a thief to catch a thief -English, French
Set out wisely at first; custom will make every virtue more easy and
pleasant to you than any vice can be -English
Set thy expense according to thy trade -Dutch
Set your sail [according] to the wind -French
Setting out well is a quarter of the journey -French
*Settle quarrels soon, for harmony is best- Lawsuits eat time, friends,*
*money, and your rest*
Seven trades but no luck
Several eyes see more than only one -Latin
Sex is an emotion in motion -Mae West
Shady business brings/gives not a sunny life
*Shady business, frequent strife- never give a sunny life*
Shall the gosling teach the goose to swim?
Shallow streams make most din
Shame comes to no man unless he himself help it on the way -Danish
Shame is easier to bear than smoke in the eyes -Russian
Shame lasts longer than poverty -Dutch
Shame when you ask is less than when you didn't -Japanese
Shame with profit beats pride with poverty -Ferengi Rule of Acquisition
Shameful deeds bring on revenge -Norwegian
Share not pears with your master, either in jest or in earnest
Share your wisdom, not your prejudice
Shared joy is a double joy; shared sorrow is half a sorrow -Swedish
*Shared joy is doubled joy* -Danish
*Shared pain is half pain* –Dutch
*Shared sorrow is half sorrow* -Danish
Sharing and giving are the ways of the Creator  –Sauk
*Sharing joy is the ultimate joy* -Chinese
Sharp stomachs make short graces
She can touch your lobes, but never your Gold -Ferengi Rule of
Acquisition
She hangs out the broom [wants a husband] -Dutch

She is neither fish, nor flesh, nor good red herring  —John Heywood
She is well married who has neither mother-in-law nor sister-in-law
-Portuguese
She stoops to conquer -Portuguese
She that is born a beauty is half married
She who does not yet know how to walk cannot climb a ladder -Ethiopian
She who is born a beauty is born betrothed -Italian
Shear the sheep but don't flay them -Dutch
Sheep stay away from wolves, and for good reason
Shew me a man without a spot, and I'll shew you a maid without a fault
Shoemakers are always the worst shod -French
Short accounts make long friends
*Short acquaintance brings repentance* -English
*Short cheerful meals in silence, music and a healthy conscience would*
*you reach healthy, happy age*
Short flax makes long thread -Danish
Short folk are soon angry
Short hair is combed in a moment
Short is my date, but deathless my renown
Short pleasure often brings long repentance -Danish
Short pleasure, long repentance
Short pleasures may bring long pain
Should the heavens fall, many pipkins will be broken -Danish
Show him death, and he will be content with fever -Arabic
Show me a liar and I will show you a thief
Show me a poor man, I will show you a flatterer -Portuguese
Show me the person who never makes a mistake and I'll show you the
person who never makes anything
Show respect for all men, but grovel to none  —Shawnee
Show the fatted calf, but not what fatted it -Irish
Show them your strength, and they take notice.  Show them your
weakness, and they take.
Shrouds are made without pockets -Yiddish
Shun not the struggle; face it
Shut your door, and you will make your neighbour good -Portuguese
Shut your mouth and you'll catch no flies -Portuguese
Sick people are like kings -Madagasy
Sickness comes in haste, and goes at leisure -Danish
Sickness comes on horseback and departs/goes away on foot -Dutch
Sickness comes uninvited--no need to bespeak it -Danish
Sickness is a teacher like old age, it teaches us about life, and
perspective, and impermanence, and the future
Sickness is every man's master -Danish

Sickness is felt, but health not at all
Sickness shows us what we are
Sickness soaks the purse
Sight goes before hearsay -Danish
Silence answers much -Dutch
Silence does seldom harm
Silence gives consent -German, Latin
Silence has so much meaning -Yurok
Silence in times of suffering is the best
Silence is a fence around wisdom -Hebrew
Silence is a fine jewel for a woman, but it is little worn -Hebrew
Silence is a friend that will never betray you -Confucius
Silence is a great treasure
Silence is a woman's best garment -Hebrew
Silence is an attribute of the dead; he who is alive speaks -Yoruba
Silence is consent
Silence is golden, [speech is silver]
Silence is learnt by the misfortunes of life
Silence is more eloquent than words
Silence is not always a Sign of Wisdom, but Babbling is ever a folly - Ben Franklin
*Silence is often misinterpreted but never misquoted*
Silence is often the best answer
Silence is one of the hardest arguments to refute
Silence is one of the most effective forms of communication
Silence is sometimes the answer -Estonian
Silence is sometimes the severest criticism
Silence is the fittest reply to folly
Silence is the hardest argument to refute
Silence was never written down -Italian
Silent gratitude isn't much good to anyone -Gladys Browyn Stern
Silent men, like still waters, are deep and dangerous
Silent tongue and hempen heart often go together -Danish
Silks and satins put out the fire in the kitchen
Silver and gold are all men's dears -Danish
*Simple hugs do warm the heart    for welcoming, and when we part*
Simplicity, color, celebration, and beauty feed the spirit
Sin and sorrow are inseparable
Sin is energy in the wrong channel -St. Augustine
Sin is not allowed in God's longhouse  –Mohawk
Sin is not hurtful because it is forbidden but it is forbidden because it is hurtful -Ben Franklin
Since nature cannot change, true friendships are eternal -Horatius

Since the house is on fire I will warm myself at the blaze -Italian
Since the house is on fire let us warm ourselves -Italian
Since the wine is drawn it must be drunk -French
Since we cannot get what we like, let us like what we can get -Spanish
Since when do you have to agree with people to defend them from injustice?   -Lillian Hellman
Sincerity, a deep genuine, heart-felt sincerity, is a trait of true and noble manhood
Sing away sorrow, cast away care -Miguel de Cervantes
Sing your death song and die like a hero going home  –Shawnee
Singers, poets, and lovers are privileged liars
Sink or swim
Sit a beggar at your table and he will soon put his feet on it -Russian
Sit at the feet of the masters long enough, and they'll start to smell
Sit on the bank of a river and wait: Your enemy's corpse will soon float by - Indian
Sit, Rest, Work. Alone with yourself, never weary. On the edge of the forest live joyfully, without desire -Buddha
Sit squarely in the saddle -Dutch
Sitting is being crippled -Ethiopian
Sitting quietly, doing nothing, spring comes and the grass grows by itself -Zen
Six feet of earth make us all equal -Italian
Six hours' sleep for a man, seven for a woman and eight for a fool -English, Italian
Six of one, and half a dozen of the other -Italian, English
Six things have no business in the world: a fighting priest, a coward knight, a covetous judge, a stinking barber, a soft-hearted mother, and an itchy baker -French
Skeptics are never deceived -French
Skill and assurance are an invincible couple
Skill and confidence are an unconquered army
Skill or fortune will efface the spots -Italian
Skills can be taught, attitude cannot
Slander expires at a good woman's door -Danish
Slander leaves a score behind it -Danish
Slander slays three persons: the speaker, the spoken to, and the spoken of -Hebrew
Slander! slander! some of it always sticks -French
Slanderers are the devil's bellows, to blow up contention -French
Sleep after selling horses and elephants - Hindi
Sleep can interfere with profit -Ferengi Rule of Acquisition
Sleep tight, don't let the bedbugs bite - Colonial American

Sleeping is the best cure for waking troubles
Sleeping people can't fall down -Japanese
Sleeping shrimp get taken by the current  —Puerto Riqueño
Sloth is the beginning of vice -Dutch
Sloth is the key to poverty
Sloth turneth the edge of wit
Sloth, like rust, consumes faster than labour wears
Slow and steady forward motion will always get you to your destination
Slow and steady wins the race -Aesop
Slow but sure
Slow help is no help
Slowly but surely
Slowly one goes far -Portuguese
Slowly, the file turns the beam into a needle -Albanian
Smack a tray of water, and you get to wash your face -Malay
Small and smart is worthwhile, too
Small articles come in big packages
Small beer comes the last -Danish
Small brooks make the greatest noise
Small children give you a headache, big children a heartache - Russian
Small choice in rotten apples -Russian
Small deeds done are better than great deeds planned
Small faults indulged in are little thieves that let in greater -Russian
Small gains bring great wealth -Dutch
*Small men imitate, great men originate*
Small ones never differ
Small opportunities are often the beginning of great enterprises  —
Demosthenes
*Small pots have big ears, as children grow with passing years*
Small print leads to large risk -Ferengi Rule of Acquisition
Small profits are sweet -Danish
Small rain lays a great wind -Italian
Small rain lays great dust -Italian
Small sorrows speak; great ones are silent
Small talk is sufficient for little men
*Small thieves find themselves soon jailed, while great ones, feted, are soon hailed*
*Small thieves are by neck soon hung; great thieves have their praises sung*
Small tubs have ears, too
Smile and the world smiles with you- cry and you cry alone
Smile when picking up the phone. The caller will hear it in your voice.
Smile, it's free therapy -Doug Horton

Smiles open many doors
*Smoke, floods, and a troublesome wife, are enough to drive a man out of his life* -French
*Smoke, rain, and a scolding wife, are three bad things in  house and life*
Smokey chimney and scolding wife are bad companions in one's life
Smoking helps you lose weight -- one lung at a time!
Smooth hands love the labor of others -Russian
Smooth seas do not make skillful sailors -African
Smooth water runs deep
Smooth words do not flay the tongue -Italian
Smooth words make smooth ways -Italian
Snapping curs never want sore ears -Italian
Snarling curs never want sore ears -French
Snivelling folks always want to wipe other folks' noses -French
Snuff at a wake is fine if there's nobody sneezing over the snuff box -Irish
So good that he is good for nothing -Italian
So got, so gone -Dutch
So ignorant, that he bought a cow to ride on - Ben Franklin
So long as it's here, there's no remedy for fear
So many countries, so many customs -Italian
So many heads, so many brains -Italian
So many heads, so many minds -Danish
So many *little* things makes a man love a woman in a *BIG* way -Ghana
So many men, so many opinions
So many men/or heads so many minds/or wits
So many servants, so many enemies
So much is mine as I enjoy
*So once was I as now art thee- as I am now, so shalt thou be* [Eram quod es, eris quod sum]
*Sodom apples outwardly fair, ashes at the core* -Polish
Soft and fair goeth far -Dutch
Soft doctors make smelly wounds  –Dutch [Better to treat painfully and fix it now, rather than let it fester]
Soft fire makes sweet malt -English
Soft is the heart of a child; do not harden it
Soft pace goes far
Soft water constantly striking the hard stone, wears it at last -Portuguese
*Soft water on hard stone- will a hole within it hone*
Soft words and hard arguments -Portuguese
Soft words butter no parsnips, but they won't harden the heart of the cabbage either -Irish
Soft words scald not the tongue -French
Soft/Fine/Kind words butter no parsnips [but the meal tastes better with

them]
Softly, barber, the water scalds -Italian
Softly, don't raise a dust -Italian
*Softly, softly, catchee monkey*
Soldiers fight, and the kings are heroes
Solitude is fine, but it's usually more fun enjoying it with somebody else
*Solutions come to calmer spirit- in the silence you will hear it*
Solutions flow to the most calm as water flows to the lowest point
Solutions that are fun for all are the right solutions -Wampanoag
Some [writing] is praised, but other is read -Latin
Some are smart, but they are not wise  –Shoshone
*Some are weatherwise, some are otherwise* - Ben Franklin
*Some books are to be tasted, others to be swallowed, and some few to be chewed and digested*
Some cause happiness wherever they go; others, whenever they go - Oscar Wilde
Some chores have to be put off many times before they slip your mind completely
Some folks wear their halos much too tight
Some go through life as freight. They can't seem to express themselves.
Some have been thought brave because they were afraid to run away Ralph Waldo Emerson
Some have bread who have no teeth left -French
Some have fine eyes and can't see a jot -French
Some marriages are made in heaven, but they ALL have to be maintained on earth
Some men go through a forest and see no firewood -English
Some men have only one book in them, others a library -English
Some men see things as they are and ask Why? I dream of things that never were and ask Why not? -J.  F. Kennedy
Some minds are like concrete, thoroughly mixed up and permanently set
Some mistakes are too much fun to only make once
Some of the sweetest berries grow among the sharpest thorns -Gaelic
Some people are kind, polite, sweet and spiritual, until you try to sit in their pews
Some people are like blisters. They don't show up until the work is done.
Some people are like buttons--always popping off at the wrong time
Some people are masters of money, and some its slaves -Russian
Some people are no good at counting calories and have the figures to prove it
Some people cannot see the wood for the trees
Some people do odd things to get even
Some people get their exercise by jumping to conclusions

*Some people give and forgive; Others get and forget*
Some people give their worries swimming lessons, instead of drowning them
Some people go into debt trying to keep up with people who are already there
Some people grow under responsibility. Other people merely swell.
Some people have good aim, but fail to pull the trigger
Some people have tact, others tell the truth
Some people learn from books, some from other people.  The vast majority of people have to pee on the electric fence –Will Rogers
Some people make things happen, some watch things happen, while others wonder what happened, and some have no clue whatsoever. – Gaelic, Joseph Patterson
Some people never change their opinion because it's been in the family for generations
*Some people stand for nothing because they fall for everything*
Some people talk like a book, but you can't shut them up as easily
Some people think they are generous because they give away free advice
Some persons do first, think afterwards, and then repent for ever
Some revelations show best in a twilight -Herman Melville
Some sell and don't deliver -French
Some sing who are not merry -Italian
*Some succeed because they are destined to, but most succeed because they were determined to*
Some there are that torment themselves afresh with the memory of what is past; others, again, afflict themselves with the apprehension of evils to come; and very ridiculously both - for the one does not now concern us, and the other not yet .... One should count each day a separate life -Seneca
Some things are better left unsaid
Some things have to be believed to be seen -Ralph Hodgson
Some things just don't need all the thought that people invest in them
Some think they have done when they are only beginning -French
Some thinking to avenge their shame increase it -French
Some who just tell tales of themselves -Italian
Some who mean only to warm, burn themselves -French
Something is better than nothing -French
Sometimes an egg is given for an ox -Italian
Sometimes being true to yourself means disappointing others
Sometimes dreams are wiser than waking -Oglala
Sometimes I go about pitying myself, and all the time I am being carried on great wings across the sky -Ojibwa

Sometimes I wonder whether the world is being run by smart people who are putting us on, or by imbeciles who really mean it -Mark Twain
*Sometimes in pity for myself, go I- while a great wind bears me across the sky* -Ojibwa
Sometimes it is better to give your apple away, than to eat it yourself -Italian
Sometimes problems are more elusive than solutions
Sometimes the best gain is to lose
Sometimes the best thing to get off your chest is your chin
Sometimes the fool who rushes in gets the job done -Al Bernstein
Sometimes the highest mountain brings forth the smallest mouse -Russian
Sometimes the lees are better than the wine -Italian
Sometimes the only thing more dangerous than a question is an answer -Ferengi Rule of Acquisition
Sometimes the remedy is worse than the disease -Francis Bacon
Sometimes words hurt more than swords
Sometimes you already have what you pray for
Sometimes you get, and sometimes you get got -Country Wisdom
Sometimes you lose a forest through the trees -Chinese
Sometimes you need to take off your saddle, take out the bit, and just let the coyote inside you howl
Sometimes, it's too little, too late
Sometimes, less is more - William Shakespeare
Somewhere, something incredible is waiting to be known
Son, when you participate in sporting events, it's not whether you win or lose: it's how drunk you get -Homer Simpson
*Song may inspire and words may embolden, but it is still true that silence is golden*
Sons who want to follow in their father's footsteps shouldn't wear loafers
*Soon crooks the tree That good gambrel would be* -Italian
*Soon enough if well enough* -French
Soon fire, soon ashes -Dutch
*Soon gained, soon squandered* -French
Soon gotten, soon spent
Soon grass, soon hay -Dutch
Soon learnt, soon forgotten
Soon ripe, soon rotten -German
Soon ripe, soon rotten; soon wise, soon foolish -Dutch
Soon up, soon down
Sooner or later, the truth comes to light -Dutch
Sooner or later, all smokers quit.  Heavy smokers often quit earlier.
Sooner or later, the truth comes to light

Sorrow comes unset for
Sorrow doesn't kill, reckless joy does -Yoruba
Sorrow for a husband is like a pain in the elbow, sharp and short
Sorrow is at parting, if at meeting there be laughter
Sorrow is like rice in an attic: you use a little every day and at the end it is all gone -Madagasy
Sorrow is to the soul, as worm is to wood -Turkish
Sorrow looks back, worry looks around, and faith looks up
Sorrow seldom comes alone -Danish
Sorrow treads upon the heels of mirth
Sorrow will pay no debts -Dutch
Sorrows can't be drowned.   They know how to swim.
Sound love is not soon forgotten
Sow a thought, reap an act, sow an act, reap a habit, sow a habit reap a character, sow a character, reap a destiny - Samuel Smiles
Sow not money on the sea, lest it sink -Dutch
*Sow nothing, reap nothing*
*Sow the wind and reap the whirlwind*
*Sow thin and mow thin*
Sow with one hand, reap with both -Albanian
Spare at the spigot, and let out the bunghole -Dutch
Spare the rod and spoil the child -Biblical
Spare to speak and spare to speed -French
Spare well and have to spend -French
*Spare well and have well*
Spare when you're young and spend when you're old
Spare your breath to cool your porridge -Cervantes
*Sparing is the first gaining*
Sparrows should not dance with cranes, their legs are too short -Danish
*Speak clearly if you speak at all, carve every word before you let it fall*
*Speak fitly, or be silent wisely*
Speak less and listen more
Speak little and well, they will think you somebody -Portuguese
Speak little of your ill luck, and boast not of your good luck -Danish
Speak little, do much -Ben Franklin
Speak not of my debts unless you mean to pay them -English
Speak of angels and you will hear their wings
Speak of the devil and he appears -Italian
Speak sweetly, like the nightingale -Persian
Speak the truth and embarrass the devil
Speak the truth in humility to all people.  Only then can you be a true man -Dakota
*Speak the truth, and act on it -as soon as it comes to your spirit* -Alan

Cohen
Speak the truth, but leave immediately after -Slovenian
Speak well of the dead
Speak well of your enemies; remember that you made them
Speak well of your friend, of your enemy say nothing
Speak well of your friend; of your enemy neither well nor ill -Italian
Speak when you are spoken to -Italian
Speaking is silver, silence is gold -Dutch
Speaking silence is better than senseless speech -Danish
Speaking without thinking is shooting without taking aim
Speech is hard, but who can keep quiet?
Speech is oft[en] repented, silence seldom/never -Danish
Speech is silver, but silence is golden -Danish
Speech is silver, humor is gold
Speech is silvern, silence is golden
Speech is the picture of the mind
Speech may be silver but silence is golden
Speech shows what a man is
Speeches pass away, but acts remain -Napoleon
Speed is the soldier's asset
Speedy execution is the mother of good fortune -Danish
Spend more time figuring out what's right, than who's right -Country wisdom
Spend not all you have, believe not all you hear, tell not all you know, do not all you can
Spend some time alone
*Spend your money, as you go, with shoes worn down, at heel and toe*
Spending is quick, earning is slow -Russian
*Spice is black, but it has a sweet smack*
Spilled water from a cup returns not to the tray -Japanese
Spilt salt is never well collected -Portuguese
Spinner, spin softly, you disturb me; I am praying -Portuguese
Spit not in the well, you may have to drink its water -French
*Spit not into well or sink, lest later, from it, need ye drink* -Russian
Spoil/Lose the ship for half penny worth of tar
Spread the table and contention will cease -English
Spring appears and we are once more children
Spring has come when you can put your foot on three daisies -English
Spring is in the air
Spring is when you feel like whistling even with a shoe full of slush -English
Squander neither pity nor strength
St. Francis shaved himself first, and then he shaved his brethren -Italian

St. Peter asked the saint where he wanted to spend eternity. "In hell", he replied. "They need me there so much more."

Stability itself is nothing more than a more sluggish motion –Montaigne

Stairs are climbed step by step -Kurdish

Stand for something, or you'll fall for anything

Stand in the light when you want to speak out -Crow

Standers-by see more than gamesters

Standing in the middle of the road is dangerous. You will get knocked down by the traffic from both ways.

Standing pools gather filth -Portuguese

Starlings are lean because they go in flocks -Italian

Starry nights are good for the soul

Stars are not seen by sunshine -Spanish

Stars are not seen where the sun shines

Start by doing what is necessary; then do what is possible; and suddenly you are doing the impossible -St. Francis of Assisi

*Start out somewhere, now begin- would you success and vict'ry win*

*Start to count flowers, and cease to count weeds. When we count blessings, we cease to count needs.*

Starved lice bite the hardest -Dutch

Statistics are no substitute for judgment -Henry Clay

Statistics Means Never Having to Say You're Certain

*Stay a while, and lose a mile -Dutch*

*Stay at home, don't you roam, cause it's cheaper to keep her*

Stay neutral in conflict so that you can sell supplies to both sides -Ferengi Rule of Acquisition

Stealing from one book is plagiarism, stealing from many is research

Step after step, the ladder is ascended

Step by step one goes far -Dutch

Step by step one goes to Rome -Italian

Step lightly in the hovels of the poor- the lion sleeps in a den of rushes -Afghan

Step lightly on the feet you may need to kiss later

Stern masters do not reign long -Seneca Philosophus

Stick the needle into yourself [see how it hurts] before you thrust the packing-needle into others -Turkish

Stick to your guns

Stick to your knitting

Sticks and stones may hurt my bones, but words can never harm me

Sticks and stones may break my bones, but names will never hurt me -English

Sticks like a leaf in the bath -Russian

Still he fisheth that catcheth one -English

Still water breeds vermin -Italian
Still water runs deep
Still water undermines the bank -Russian
Still waters are deep -Dutch
Still waters are the deepest -Polish
Still waters have deep bottoms
Still waters run deep
Stock-fish are made tender by much beating -Dutch
Stolen bread stirs the appetite -French
Stolen food never satisfies hunger –Omaha
Stolen fruit is sweet -French
Stolen pleasures are sweet
Stolen waters are sweet, and bread eaten in secret is pleasant Bible -
Proverbs 9:17
Stolen waters are sweet -French
Stones decay, words last - Samoan
Stones or bread, one must have something in hand for the dogs -Italian
Stoop, and let it pass; the storm will have its way -Danish
Stop and smell the roses -Danish, English
Stop playing seriously and seriously play
Stop repeat offenders. Don't re-elect them!
Stop, look and listen -Danish
Storing milk in a sieve, you complain of bad luck? -Afghan
Straight trees have crooked roots
Strain not your bow beyond its bent, lest it break -Dutch
Strangers are friends you haven't met yet -Will Rogers
Strangers are just friends waiting to happen
*Strangers' meat is the greatest treat* -Danish
Straws tell which way the wind blows -Danish
Strength avails not a coward -Italian
Strength is law -French
Strength is lost due to youthly vices, not the ravages of age
Stress management begins by turning off the television, especially the
news -American stress management trainers
Stretch your arm no further than your sleeve will reach -Italian
Stretch your legs according to your clothes -Russian
Stretch your legs as far as your quilt allows  [Don't overreach]-Arabic
Stretch your legs no farther than your coverlet -Dutch
Strew no roses before swine -Dutch
*Strike the first blow, it's as good as two*
Strike the iron while it is hot
Strike the serpent's head with your enemy's hand
Strike while the iron is hot -Chaucer

Strive to be a person who is never absent from an important act –Osage
Strong is the vinegar of sweet wine -Italian
Strong reasons make strong actions
Study depends on the good will of the student, a quality that cannot be secured by compulsion -Latin
Study sickness while you are well
Study to be what you wish to seem
Stupid is as stupid does -Eric Roth
Stupid questions are better than stupid mistakes -Japanese
Stupidity is a disease without a medicine -Arabic
Stupidity is the only sin in nature. Judgement is swift; the punishment harsh. And there is no appeal. You live and you learn, or you don't live long.
Subtlety is the art of saying what you think and getting out of the way before it is understood
Success always occurs in private, and failure in full view
Success and rest don't sleep together -Russian
Success at first may undo a man at last
Success belongs to the persevering
Success comes in cans. Failure comes in can'ts.
Success comes to many men because they were deprived of advantages others had
Success consecrates the foulest crimes -Russian
*Success depends on your backbone, not your wishbone*
Success grows out of struggles to overcome difficulties
Success has a hundred/many fathers, while failure is an orphan -Russian
Success has many friends -Greek
Success has many parents but failure is an orphan - American
Success has ruined many a man -Ben Franklin
Success is a journey, not a destination
Success is doing what you like and making a living at it -Greek
*Success is never final and failure is never fatal*
*Success is not position won, but obstacles you've overcome*
Success is nothing more than a few simple disciplines, practiced every day - Jim Rohn
Success is often just an idea anyway
Success is simply a matter of luck.  Ask any failure.
Success isn't how far you got, but the distance you traveled from where you started -Greek
Success of the wicked entices many more
Success requires fewer blocks and a lot more tackle
Success seems to be connected with action. Successful people keep moving. They make mistakes, but they don't quit - Conrad Hilton

Successful people do the extra small things no-one else wants to do
Successful people never have to go to the bathroom
*Such beginning, such ending*
Such carpenters, such chips
Such is life! -German
Sudden power is apt to be insolent, sudden liberty saucy; that behaves best which has grown gradually - Ben Franklin
Suffer and expect
Suffering and patience, obedience and application, help the lowly born to honour -Danish
Sufficient for the day is the evil thereof -French
Sugared words soon prove bitter
Suit the action to the word
Sum up at night what thou hast done by day -George Herbert
Sun is good for cucumbers, rain for rice -Vietnamese
Supper is soon served up in a plentiful house -Portuguese
Supple as a glove -Dutch
Suppressing a moment of anger may save a day of sorrow
*Sure bind, sure find*
Surely thou jivest...
Surfeits slay mae[more] than swords -Scots
Surmounted labours are pleasant -Latin
Suspicion is the poison of friendship -French
Suspicion is the sister of the wrong -Arabic
Sussex won't be druv -English
Swallows and sparrows cannot understand the ambitions of swans
Sweep before your own door before you look after your neighbour's -Dutch
Sweep in front of your own door -English
Sweet are the slumbers of a virtuous man - Joseph Addison
Sweet are the uses of adversity
Sweet discourse makes short days and nights
Sweet is the memory of past labor -Greek
Sweet is the wine but sour is the payment -Irish
Sweet meat requires sour sauce -Italian
Swift gratitude is the sweetest -Greek
Swim on and don't trust -French
Sympathy is found between shit and syphilis, in the dictionary -Richard Marcinko, Richard Schulze
Sympathy is never wasted except when you give it to yourself
*Tact is the ability to describe others as they see themselves -Abraham Lincoln*
Tact is the ability to tell a man he has an open mind when he has a hole

in his head
Take a dog for a companion and a stick in your hand -English
Take a hair of the dog that has bitten you -English
Take a horse by his bridle and a man by his word -Dutch
Take a little time to do whatever makes a happy you
Take a pain for a pleasure all wise men can
Take a risk a day – one small or bold stroke that will make you feel great
once you have done it -Susan Jeffers
Take a woman's first advice and not her second -French
Take advice of a red-bearded man, and be gone -Danish
Take all you want, eat all you take -German, English
Take an eel in hand, a woman at her word; little stays in your hand
-Russian
Take an ox by his horn, a man by his word -French
Take away fuel, take away flame -French
Take away my good name, take away my life -French
Take care how you beseech the gods for a gift, for they will give it to you
Take care how you beseech the gods, they may answer you
Take care of small sums and the large will take care of themselves
Take care of the little things, and the big things take care of themselves
Take care of the minutes and the hours will take care of themselves -
Phillip Dormer Stanhope, Earl of Chesterfield
Take care of the pence and the pounds will take care of themselves
Take care of the sense, and the sounds will take care of themselves
Take care of your geese when the fox preaches -Danish
Take care of your pennies and your pounds will take care of your heirs
and barristers -English
*Take care to whom you tell your goal and never, ever, show your roll*
Take care you don't let your tail be caught in the door -Italian
Take counsel before it goes ill, lest it go worse -Dutch
Take counsel of/consult with one's pillow
Take down a rogue from the gallows and he will hang you up -French,
Italian
Take gifts with a sigh; most men give to be paid -Irish
*Take heed is a good reed* -Irish
Take heed of an enemy reconciled -French
Take heed of an ox before, an ass behind, and a monk on all sides
-French
Take heed of enemies reconciled, and of meat twice boiled -English
Take heed of still waters, the quick pass away
Take help of many, advice of few -Danish
*Take hikes and fly more kites*
Take honour from me and my life is undone

Take it straight from the horse's mouth - Francis Iles
Take it with a grain of salt -Plinius the Elder
Take life as it comes
Take little, but give much
Take no more on you than you're able to bear
Take not your sickle to another man's corn -Danish
Take nothing in hand that may bring repentance -Dutch
Take off your hat to your yesterdays; take off your coat for your tomorrows -Dutch
Take one thing with another
Take one's courage in both hands
Take only what you need, and leave the land as you found it –Arapaho
Take something by the best handle
Take the bull by the horns -North American
Take the chestnuts out of the fire with the cat's paw -Portuguese
Take the goods the gods provide -Russian
Take the mouth to the bread, not the bread to the mouth -Albanian
Take the nuts from the fire with the dog's foot
Take the rough with the smooth
Take the world as it is
Take the world as one finds it
Take things always by their smooth handle –Thomas Jefferson
Take things as they come/are
Take thy thoughts to bed with thee, for the morning is wiser than the evening -Russian
Take time by the forelock
Take time do do what you love, or what you love will be lost in time
Take time for deliberation; haste spoils everything
Take time to deliberate; but when the time for action arrives, stop thinking and go in
Take time to smell the roses -Russian
Take time when time comes lest time steal away
Take time when time is, for time will away -Russian
Take your children with you where you go and be not ashamed -Hopi
Take your eyes off your watch and watch more with your eyes
Take your hat off to the past; take your coat off to the future
Take your life in your own hands, and what happens? A terrible thing: no one to blame -Erica Jong
Taking a moment to take it easy is being a friend to yourself
Taking out without putting in, soon comes to the bottom -Portuguese
Taking the first step with the good thought, the second with the good word, and the third with the good deed, I enter paradise -Persian
Taking the snake to school is one thing, making it sit is another -Haitian

Talent creates its own opportunities. Intense desire can create not only its own, but for others also.

Talented hawks hide their nails - Japanese

Talk is cheap

Talk of an angel and you'll hear his wings

Talk of the devil - and the devil appears

Talk of the devil and he is sure to appear -English, Dutch, Rumanian

Talk of the devil and he will appear

Talk of the devil and you hear his bones rattle -Dutch

Talk of the wolf and behold his skin -Portuguese

Talk of the wolf and his tail appears -Dutch, French, Rumanian

Talk slowly but think quickly

Talk to your children while they are eating, what you say will stay even after you are gone -Nez Perce

Talk was given to the people for good –Sauk

Talking about it won't help you reduce. You have to keep your mouth shut

Talking is silver, silence is golden -French

Talking mends no holes

Tall mankind are beholden to him that is kind to the good

Tall trees catch much wind -Dutch

Tap even a stone bridge before crossing it -Korean

Taste your words before you spit them out

Tastes differ -Dutch

Taxation WITH representation isn't so hot, either!

Teach not fish to swim

Teach others by your example

Teach thy tongue to say, "I do not know" - Hebrew

Teach your grandam to spin - Hebrew

Teach your grandame to suck eggs - Hebrew

Teachers not only teach, they also learn –Sauk

Teachers open the door, but you must enter by yourself -Chinese

Teachers, Moms, and hoot owls sleep with one eye open

Teaching others teaches yourself

Teaching others teacheth yourself

Tears are the silent language of grief

Tears dry quickly, especially when they are for others' misfortunes -Latin

Teenagers act like babies if they're not treated like adults

Teenagers get confused when some advise: Find yourself, while others say: Get lost.

Teeth placed before the tongue give good advice -Italian

Television has proved that people will look at anything rather than each other -Ann Landers

Tell everybody your business and the devil/they will do it for you -Italian

Tell God the truth, but give the judge money -Russian
Tell her she is handsome, and you will turn her brain -Portuguese
Tell it to the marines
Tell lies, but become not tangled in lies -Russian
Tell me and I'll forget. Show me, and I may not remember. Involve me, and I'll understand -Native American, Confucius
Tell me thy company and I will tell thee what thou art
Tell me who you associate with, and I will tell you who you are -German
Tell me who you live with and I will tell you who you are -Spanish
Tell me whom you associate with, and I will tell you who you are
Tell me whom you love and I'll tell you who you are - African-American
Tell me who's your friend and I'll tell you who you are -Russian
*Tell me with whom thou goest, and I'll tell thee what thou doest* -Portuguese/English/Slavic
Tell no one what you would have known only to yourself -Dutch
Tell not all you know nor judge of all you see if you would live in peace
Tell nothing to thy friend which why enemy may not know -Danish
Tell tales out of school  –John Heywood
Tell the truth and shame the devil
Tell your friend your secret, and he will set his foot on your neck -Portuguese, Italian
Tell your friends a lie; if he keeps it secret tell him the truth -Portuguese
*Telling your troubles is swelling your troubles*
Temper is so good a thing that we should never lose it
Temper justice with mercy - John Milton
Temperance is reason's girdle and passion's bridle
Temperance is the best medicine/physic -Italian
Temperance is the greatest of virtues
Tempest in a teapot
Ten no's are better then one lie -Danish
Ten pounds of oxtail makes a good soup
Tender surgeons make foul wounds -Dutch
Terrifying are the weaknesses of power -Greek
Thank who gives to you and give to who thanks you -Arabic
Thank you, pretty pussy, was the death of my cat -Italian
Thanks cost nothing -Creole
That beer's of your own brewing, and you must drink it -Dutch
That bench is well adorned that is filled with virtuous women -Danish
That costs dear which is bought with begging -Italian
That day is lost on which one has not laughed -French
That feeling isn't fear, it's just telling you to MOVE!!
That happens in a moment which may not happen in a hundred years -Italian

That is a good book which is opened with expectation and closed with profit

That is beggar's fare, said the dame, when she fried eggs with the sausages -Dutch

That is certain that can be made certain -Latin

That is done soon enough which is well done -Italian

That is good wisdom which is wisdom in the end -Dutch

That is not good language which all understand not

That is pleasant to remember which was hard to endure -Italian

That is poor help that helps you from the feather-bed to the straw -Danish

That is true which all men say -Danish

That land fares ill where the king's but a babe

That may be soon done, which brings long repentance -Danish

That mouse will have a tail[a long train of consequences] -Dutch

That often happens in a day which does not happen in a hundred years -French

That priest is a fool who decries his relics -Italian

That suit is best that best fits me -Italian

That teacher helps his pupils most who most helps them to help themselves

That that comes of a cat will catch mice -Italian

That was indeed a pretty kettle of fish

That which burns thee not, cool not -Dutch

That which comes of a cat will catch mice -Slavic

That which comes with sin, goes with sorrow -Danish

That which has been eaten out of the pot cannot be put into the dish -Danish

That which has been thrown away has often to be begged for again -Danish

That which is customary requires no excuse -Italian

That which is evil is soon learnt

That which is stamped a penny will never be a pound -Danish

That which is striking and beautiful is not always good, but that which is good is always beautiful

That which is unsaid, may be spoken; that which is said, cannot be unsaid -Danish

That which must be, will be -Danish

*That which one least anticipates soonest comes to pass*

That which one most forgets soonest comes to pass

*That which was bitter to endure may be sweet to remember*

That's where the shoe pinches. That's the crux/rub.

That's all well and good, but gold is better -Dutch

That's but an empty purse which is full of other men's money -Danish

That's good wisdom which is wisdom in the end
That's quickly done which is long repented -Dutch
Thaw reveals what has been hidden by snow -Danish
The abbey does not fail for want on one monk -French
The absent always bear the blame -Dutch
The absent are always to blame/in the wrong
The abundance of money ruins youth
The accomplice is as bad as the thief -Portuguese
The adult looks to deeds, the child to love - Hindi
The afternoon knows what the morning never expected -Swedish
The afterthought is good for nought, except it be to catch blind horses with -English
The afterthought is good, but forethought is better -Norwegian
The age of miracles is past -Norwegian
The aged in council--the young in action -Danish
The aim of life is to live, and to live means to be aware, joyously, drunkenly, serenely, divinely aware -Henry Miller
The anger of the prudent never shows -Burmese
The angry man defeats himself in battle as well as in life -Samurai
The answer to the question: "What is the meaning of life and the universe?" is: 42
The ant preaches the best sermon, yet she is silent
The anvil does not fear a good sledge-hammer -Danish
The anvil fears no blows -Polish,Romanian
The anvil lasts longer than the hammer -Italian
The appetite comes during a meal
The applause of the people is a blast of air -Italian
The apple doesn't fall far from the tree –German, English
*The archer that shoots badly has a lie ready* -Portuguese
The arguments of the strongest have always the most weight -French
The arm of the moral universe is long, but it bends towards justice -Dr. Martin Luther King
The arms of Bruges: an ass in an arm-chair -Dutch
The arrogance of age must submit to be taught by youth -Edmund Burke
The art is not in making money, but in keeping it -Dutch
The art of conversation lies in the ability to disagree without being disagreeable
–Minquass
The art of giving is perfected through anonymity -Doug Horton
The ass and the driver never think alike -Dutch
The ass dead, the corn at his tail -Portuguese
The ass does not know the value of his tail till he has lost it –Portuguese, Italian

The ass embraced the thistle, and they found themselves relations -Portuguese

The ass of many owners is eaten by wolves -Portuguese

The ass that is common property is always the worst saddled -French

The ass that is hungry eats thistles -Portuguese

The ass that trespasses on a stranger's premises will leave them laden with wood [cudgelled] -Portuguese

The ass wags his ears

The ass well knows in whose house he brays -Portuguese

The ass's hide is used to the stick -Italian

The ass's son brays one hour daily -Portuguese

The assertion: It can't happen to me, keeps many from worrying themselves to death

The ax in the house spares the carpenter -German

The back door is the one that robs the home -Italian

The backbone of surprise is fusing speed with secrecy -Von Clausewitz

The bad news is, we may be lost; but the good news is, we're way ahead of schedule -David Lee Roth

The bad plowman quarrels with his ox -Korean

The bagpipe never utters a work till its belly is full -French

The bait hides the hook -English

The baker's child goes hungry -Turkish

The balance in doing its office knows neither gold nor lead -French

The barking of a dog does not disturb the man on a camel -Egyptian

The barn door is locked when the horse is gone

The battle is to the strong

The beadle of the parish is always of the vicar's opinion -French

The beadle's cow may graze in the churchyard -Dutch

The beard does not make the philosopher -Italian

The beast dead, the venom is dead -French

The beast once dead, the venom is dead -Italian

The beast that goes always never wants blows

The beast that goes well never wants a rider to try its paces -Portuguese

The beaten pay the fine -French

The beaten road is the safest

The beggar may sing before the thief

The beggar's wallet has no bottom -Italian

The beginning is the half of every action -Greek

The beginning of health is sleep -Irish

The beginning of wisdom is to call things by their right names - Chinese

The beginnings of all things are small

The believer is happy; the doubter is wise - Hungarian

The belly does not accept bail -Portuguese

The belly gives no credit -Danish
The belly has no conscience
The belly has no ears
The belly hates a long sermon
The belly is ungrateful- it always forgets we already gave it something
The belly overrules the head -French
The belly robs the back -French
The belly teaches all arts
The belly warm, the foot at rest -Portuguese
The benefice must be taken with its liabilities -French
The best advice is found on the pillow -Danish
The best always goes first -Italian
The best angle to approach a problem is from "try" angle
The best armor is to keep out of range -Italian
The best board of education is sometimes a shingle
The best candle is understanding -Welsh
The best cart may overthrow -Polish
The best cause requires a good pleader -Dutch
The best company must part, as King Dagobert said to his hounds -French
The best contract always has a lot of fine print -Ferengi Rule of Acquisition
The best cure for a short temper is a long walk
The best cure for the body is to quiet the mind -Napoleon
The best deal brings the most profit -Ferengi Rule of Acquisition
The best doctor knows the worthlessness of the most medicines -Benjamin Franklin
The best driver will sometimes upset -French
The best eraser in the world is a good night's sleep
The best fish smell when they are three days old
The best fish swim near the bottom
The best fodder is the master's eye -Dutch
The best friend is the one who does not joke around -Arabic
The best gift comes from the heart -Arabic
The best gifts are [always] tied with heartstrings
The best goods are the cheapest -Dutch
The best hearts are always the bravest
The best horse can't wear two saddles
*The best horse needs breaking, and the aptest child needs teaching*
The best horse stumbles sometimes -Dutch
The best is often[times] the enemy of the good -French, Italian
The best is the cheapest -Italian
The best is yet to come -French

The best man stumbles
The best manure is under the farmer's shoe -Danish
The best marriage counselor is the child who hugs Mom and Dad at the same time
The best memory is that which forgets nothing but injuries.  Write kindness in marble and write injuries in the dust -Persian
The best mirror is a friend's eye
The best mirror is an old friend -George Herbert
The best mode of instruction is to practice what we preach -Persian
The best of all governments is that which teaches us to govern ourselves
The best of friends must part -Persian
The best of men are but men at best -Persian
The best patch is of the same cloth
The best pears fall into the pigs' mouths -Italian
The best physicians are Dr. Diet, Dr. Quiet, and Dr. Merryman
The best pilots are ashore -Dutch
The best proof of wisdom is the result
The best remedy against an ill man is much ground between
The best remedy for anger is delay
The best safety device in a car is a rear view mirror with a policeman in it
The best sauce in the world is hunger -Miguel de Cervantes
The best sermons are lived, not preached -Country Wisdom
The best smell is bread, the best savour salt, the best love that of children
The best spices are in small bags -Italian
The best steel takes the hottest fire and the hardest blows [Yet there comes a time when the tool is forged, and ready for its purpose. So it is also with people.]
The best swimmer is the first to drown himself -Italian
The best teacher one can have is necessity
The best teachers of humanity are the lives of great men
The best thing a man can do for his kids is to love their mother
The best thing about a man is his dog -French
The best thing about telling the truth is...you don't have to remember what you said!
The best thing about the future is that it comes only one day at a time -Abraham Lincoln
The best things come in small packages
The best things in life are free -B.G. DeSilva
The best things in life are messy
The best things in life may be free, but things money can buy aren't bad either
The best throw of the dice is to throw them away -Spanish
The best trees are the most beaten -Italian

The best vitamin for making friends....B1.
The best way to be understood is to be understanding
The best way to break a bad habit is to drop it
The best way to double your money is to fold it once and put it back in your pocket -Country Wisdom
The best way to get even is to forget
The best way to keep good acts in memory is to repeat them - Cato
The best way to keep loyalty in a man's heart is to keep money in his purse -Irish
The best way to never be caught telling a lie is to never tell one
The best way to pay for a lovely moment is to enjoy it -Richard Bach
The best way to predict the future is to create/invent it - Alan Kay
The best wine has its lees -French
The best wine is that a body drinks of another man's cost -Rumanian
The best you get is an even break -French
The best-laid schemes of mice and men gang aft agley -Burns
The better lawyer, the worse Christian -Dutch
The better the day, the better the deed -Dutch
The Bible tells us to love our neighbors, and also to love our enemies; probably because generally they are the same people - Gilbert Chesterton
The big fish eat the little ones -French, Italian
The big fish is caught with big bait –Sierra Leone
The big thieves hang the little ones -Czech
The bigger the front, the bigger the back. The bigger the top, or left side, the bigger the bottom, or right side. 1 of 7 Universal Principles- George Ohsawa
The bigger the river the bigger the fish -Portuguese
The bigger the roof, the more snow [to shovel] -Farsi
The bigger the smile, the sharper the knife -Ferengi Rule of Acquisition
The bigger they are/come, the harder they fall -Portuguese
The biggest mistake you can make is to always be afraid of making one
The biggest objection to the younger generation is that many of us don't belong to it
The biggest troublemaker you'll probably ever have to deal with, watches you from the mirror every morning -Country Wisdom
The bird hunting a locust is unaware of the hawk hunting him -Portuguese
The bird is known by his note, the man by his words
The bird once out of hand is hard to recover -Danish
The bird ought not to soil its own nest -French
The bird that has eaten cannot fly with the bird that is hungry –Omaha
*The bird that's singing, without rest- will not ever make its nest* -West African

The biter is often bit -French
The biter is sometimes bit -Italian
The bitter cup we strive to remove from us holds the medicine we are most in need of -Gaelic
The blade wears out the sheath -French
The bleating of the lamb merely arouses the tiger -French
The blind man has picked up a coin -Portuguese
The blind man is laughing at the bald head -Persian
The blind person is not afraid of ghosts -Burmese
The block of wood should not dictate to the carver -Maori
The blood of the martyrs is the seed of the Church
The blunders of physicians are covered by the earth -Portuguese
The body builds up with work, the mind with studying -Albanian
The body is a house for thoughts -Hawaiian
The boor looks after a cent as the devil after a soul -Dutch
The borrower is servant to the lender -Portuguese
The bottom log comes on top
*The bough that bears most, hangs lowest*
The bow may be bent until it breaks -Danish
The bow must not be always bent -Dutch
The brains don't lie in the beard -Portuguese
The branch is seldom better than the stem -Danish
The branch must be bent early that is to make a good crook -Danish
The brave man hazards his life, but not his conscience
The brave person regards dying as going home -Chinese
The bravest are surely those who have the clearest vision of what is before them, glory and danger alike, and yet notwithstanding go out to meet it -Thucydides
The braying of an ass does not reach heaven -Portuguese, Italian
The bread eaten, the company departs -Portuguese
The bread never falls but on its buttered side -Portuguese
The brightest of all things, the sun, has its spots
The bucket goes so often to the well that it leaves its handle there -Italian
The buckets take to fighting with the well, and get their heads broken -Italian
The bud becomes a rose and the rose a hip -French
The burden on likes is cheerfully borne
The busiest men find/have the most leisure/time
The busy bee has no time to be sad
The butcher looked for his knife and it was in his mouth
*The butterfly sleeps well    Perched on the temple bell ... Until it rings* -Buson
The buyer needs a hundred eyes, the seller but one -George Herbert,

Polish
The buyer of the rotten beans is the blind man -Turkish
The calm [comes] before the storm
The calmer you go, the further along you will be -Russian
The calmest husbands make the stormiest wives -English
The camel asking for horns lost also his ears -English [In grasping for
things we need not, we often lose what we have -English]
The camel going to seek horns, lost his ears -Polish
The candle that goes before gives the best light -Dutch
The candle that goes before, is better than that which comes after
-French
The cask always smells of the herring -French
The cask can give no other wine that that it contains -Italian
The cask savours of the first fill -Portuguese
The cat and dog may kiss, yet are none the better
*The cat has nine lives: three for playing, three for straying, three for
staying* -English
The cat in gloves catches no mice -Ben Franklin, Spanish
The cat is a good friend, only she scratches -Portuguese
The cat loves fish, but is loth to wet her feet -Italian
The cat shut its eyes while it steals cream
The cat shuts its eyes when stealing
The cat well knows whose beard she licks -Portuguese
The cat would eat fish but would not get her feet wet -Chaucer
The cat's playthings are the mouse's tears -Russian
The cattle is as good as the pasture in which it grazes -Ethiopian
The cave you fear to enter holds the treasure you seek -Joseph Campbell
The chain is no stronger than its weakest link
The chamber-bell/chamber-clapper is the worst sound one have in his
ears -Italian
The chameleon changes color to match the earth, the earth doesn't
change color to match the chameleon -Senegalese
The chicken that cries at night does not lay eggs in the morning -Albanian
The chief aim of man is not to get money
The chief enemy of good is better
The chief object of education is not to learn things but to unlearn things -
G.K. Chesterton
The child has a thick skull
The child is father of/to the man
The child of a tiger is a tiger -Haitian
The child saith nothing but what he heard at the fireside
-Haitian,Portuguese
The child tells what is in the house -Albanian

The child who gets a stepmother also gets a stepfather -Danish
The child will grow, his diaper will not -Yiddish
The chip on an angry man's shoulder is often only bark
The church is an anvil which has worn out many hammers -Danish
The church is near but the road is icy; the bar is far away but I'll walk carefully -Russian, Ukranian
The church, the state, and the poor, are 3 daughters which we should maintain, but not portion off - Ben Franklin
The churl knows not the worth of spurs -French
The city of happiness is in the state of mind
The clearest sign of wisdom is continued cheerfulness -Michel de Montaigne
The clever person appears like a god and disappears like a phantom - Japanese
The clock ticks nowhere else the way it does at home -Dutch
The clothes make the man -Quintilianus
*The clothes that make a man look well- are often worn by maiden belle*
The coalheaver is master at home -French
The coat makes the man
The cobbler always wears the worst shoes -French
The cobbler must stick to his last
The cobbler's children go barefoot
The cobbler's wife is the worst shod
The cock is bold on his own dunghill -Italian
The cock often crows without a victory -Danish
The cock that crows at the wrong time is killed -Turkish
The comforter's head never aches -Italian, Slavic
The command of custom is great
The commander in the field is always right and the rear echelon is wrong -Colin Powell
The common horse is worst shod
The common soldier's blood makes the general great -Italian
The company makes the feast -J. Warton, Italian
The complete fool is half prophet - Yiddish
The concord of things through discord -Horatius
The confessed mistake is half forgiven -French
*The conflict you can quickly mend- just make your enemy your friend*
The constitution guarantees you the pursuit of happiness but doesn't guarantee to finance
The contented person can never be ruined - Chinese
The continuous drip polishes the stone -Peruvian
The control center of your life is your attitude
The corn falls out of a shaken sheaf -French

The corn that is taken to a bad mill will be badly ground -Danish
The coroner and the lawyer grow fat on the quarrels of fools -Gaelic
The cost of living hasn't affected its popularity
*The counsel thou wouldst have another keep, first thine own doings, in it steep*
The counterfeit image of a pot with two ears -Dutch
The country rooster crows not in town -Swahili
The country rooster dows not crow in the town -African
The course of true love never did run smooth
The court is most merciful when the accused is most rich -Hebrew
The court of Rome likes not sheep without wool -Italian
The covetous person is always in want -Irish
The cow has no owner -Masai
The cow is milked, not the ox; the sheep is shorn, not the horse -Danish
The cow knows not what her tail is worth until she has lost it -Danish
The cow must graze where she is tied  –Sierra Leone
The cow that does not eat with the oxen, either eats before or after them -Galician
The cow that does not go in the field gets the ax -Albanian
The coward sweats in water -Ethiopian
The cowards shoots with eyes shut –Oklahoma
The cowl/hood does not make the monk
The crab that walks too far falls into the pot -Haitian
The cream always rises to the top
The creator put fun on the earth to mark out correct solutions -Wampanoag
The Creator teaches the birds to make nests, yet the nests of all birds are not alike –Duwamish
The creditor hath a better memory than the debtor
The crow may be caged but his thoughts are in the cornfield - Belizean
The crow that mimics a cormorant is drowned -Japanese
The crow thinks her own birds fairest
The crow will find its mate -Danish
The cruelest lies are often told in silence
The crushed worm will turn
The cuckold is the last that knows of it
*The cuckoo comes in April, and stays the month of May; sings a song at midsummer, and then goes away*
The cunning wife makes her husband her apron -Romanian
The cure is worse than the disease
The curse on the hearth wounds the deepest -Danish
The customer is always right - Barry Pain
The customer is always right -Danish

The customer is always right, until you get their cash -Ferengi Rule of Acquisition

The customers are known to the shopkeepers -Kashmiri

The dainties of the great are the tears of the poor

The danger past, and God forgotten -Kashmiri

The danger past, the saint cheated -Italian

The danger today is not so much that machines will learn to think and feel but that men will cease to do so

The darkest hour is nearest the dawn

The darkest hour is only 60 minutes long

The darkest hour is that before the dawn -English

The darkest hour is/comes just before dawn -Italian

The darkest hours are just before dawn - English

The darkest place is under the candlestick

The day came when the risk it took to remain tight inside the bud was more painful than the risk it took to blossom -Anais Nin

The day has eyes; the night has ears -Scottish

The day is long to him who knows not how to use it

The day is never so holy that the pot refuses to boil -Danish

The day is short but the work is much

The day is sure to come when the cow will want her tail -Danish

The day soldiers stop bringing you their problems is the day you have stopped leading them.  They have either lost confidence that you can help them, or concluded that you do not care. Either case is a failure of leadership -Colin Powell

The day will come when the cow will have use for her tail -Irish

The day without work, the night without sleep -Albanian

The day you decide to do it, is your lucky day -Japanese

The days follow each other and are not alike -French

The dead add their strength and counsel to the living –Hopi

The dead and the absent have no friends -Portuguese

The dead are soon forgotten -French

The dead in heaven are too happy to grieve for indignities to their corpses; the dead in hell have too much else to grieve for

The dead open the eyes of the living -Portuguese

The dearer the child, the sharper must be the rod -Danish

The death that will kill a man begins as an appetite -Nigerian

The deceitful have no friends -Hindi

The deeper the sorrow the less tongue it hath -Talmud

The deeper the waters are, the more still they run -Korean

The deer hunter does not notice the mountains -Zen

The demise of a regime which seeks to stifle the freedom of expression is as inevitable as the demise of a body which seeks to stifle its own breath

Tyrants sleep with one eye open

The designer of the path is the guy standing at the end of it -Amos Jessup

The desire is the father of the thought -Dutch

The devil can cite [the] Scripture[s] for his purposes

The devil catches most souls in a golden net -German

The devil dances in empty pockets -Tudor

The devil finds work for idle hands -St. Jerome

The devil has his martyrs among men -Dutch

The devil is bad because he is old -Italian

The devil is fond of his own -Galician

The devil is good when he is pleased

The devil is known by his claws

The devil is not always at a poor man's door -French

The devil is not so black as he is painted -Russian, Dutch

The devil is not so frightful/ugly as he is painted -Russian, Italian, Portuguese

The devil knows many things because he is old

*The devil leads him by the nose who the dice too often throws* -French

The Devil longs for heaven -Arabic

The devil looks after his own - Scottish

The devil lurks behind the cross -Spanish, French, Dutch

The devil makes his Christmas pies of lawyers' tongues and clerk's fingers -Spanish

The devil makes work for idle hands

The devil may die without my inheriting his horns -French

The devil may get in by the keyhole, but the door won't let him out

The devil never grants long leases -Irish

The devil rebukes sin -French

The devil seduced Eve in Italian. Eve mislead Adam in Bohemian. The Lord scolded them both in German. Then the angel drove them from paradise in Hungarian -Polish

The devil sometimes speaks the truth

The devil take the hindmost -Dutch

The devil takes a hand in what is done in haste -Kurdish

The devil tempts all, but the idle man tempts the devil -Italian, Kurdish

The devil tempts but doesn't force - Guyanan

The devil was handsome when he was young -French

*The devil was sick, the Devil a saint would be; the Devil was well, the devil a saint was he* -French

The devil was so fond of his children that he plucked out their eyes -French

The devil will tempt Lucifer -Italian

The devil wipes his breech with poor folks' pride -Ben Franklin

The Devil's children have the Devil's luck -English

The devil's in the cards, said Sam, four aces and not a single trump -Dutch

The devil's meal turns half to bran -French

The diamonds of other countries are always the most beautiful

The dictionary is the only place where success comes before work

The die is cast - Julius Caesar

The difference between a craftsman and a workman is the last few minutes the craftsman puts into the job

The difference between ordinary and extraordinary is that little extra

The difference between Vision and a hallucination is the number of people who see it

*The difference is wide that the sheets will not decide* -English

The difficult thing is to get foot in the stirrup -Italian

The difficulty lies, not in the new ideas, but in escaping the old ones, which ramify, for those brought up as most of us have been, into every corner of our minds -John Maynard Keynes

The discontented Man finds no easy Chair - Ben Franklin

The disease built from the bowl will not be healed by a pill

The disobedient fowl obeys in a pot of soup -Nigerian

The doctor amuses the patient while nature does its work -Voltaire

The doctor is often more to be feared than the disease -French

The doctor must heal his own bald head -Persian

The doctor seldom takes physic -Italian

The doctor treats, nature heals -Latin

The dog barks and the ox feeds -Italian

The dog gets into the mill under cover of the ass -French

The dog may be wonderful prose, but only the cat is poetry -French

The dog that barks much does not bite -Turkish

The dog that barks much is never good for hunting -Portuguese

The dog that barks much, bites little -Portuguese

The dog that bites does not bark in vain -Italian

The dog that fetches will carry

The dog that has been beaten with a stick is afraid of its shadow -Italian

The dog that is forced into the woods will not hunt many deer -Danish

The dog that is quarrelsome and not strong, woe to his hide -Italian

The dog that kills wolves, is killed by wolves -Portuguese

The dog that licks ashes is not to be trusted with flour -Italian

The dog that means to bite won't bark -Italian

The dog that quits barking can get some sleep -Italian

The dog that trots finds a bone

The dog wags his tail, not for you, but for your bread -Portuguese

The dog will not get free by biting his chain -Danish

The dog's kennel is not the place to keep a sausage -Danish
The dog/wolf barks in vain at the moon
The dogs bark, but the caravan goes by/on -Arabic
The donkey scratches the donkey [Stupid and conceited people flatter each other about qualities they do not possess]
The donkey sweats so the horse can be decorated with lace -Haitian
The door of sloth is the boundary of suffering -Albanian
The doors of wisdom are never shut -Ben Franklin
The doorstep to the temple of wisdom is knowledge of our own ignorance –Benjamin Franklin
The draft that blows out a match enflames a furnace, as what prostrates a coward excites a brave man to action
The Dream drives the Action -Thomas Berry
The drop excavates the stone, not with force but by falling often -Ovidius
The drop hollows the stone, not by force, but by the frequency of its fall
The drum makes a great fuss because it is empty -Trinidadian
The drums sound better at a distance[the grass is always greener on the other side of the fence] -Hindi
The drunken man's joy is often the sober man's sorrow -Danish
The drunken mouth reveals the heart's secrets
The eagle does not catch flies - Latin, German
The eagle does not hunt flies -French
The eagle does not war against frogs -Italian
The eagle flies in the sky, but nests on the ground -Albanian
The eagle was killed with an arrow made with its own feathers - Armenian
The ear is the road to the heart -French
The early bird catches the worm - William Camden
The early bird gets the worm
The early bird may get the worm, but the second mouse gets the cheese
The early man never borrows from the late man -French
The early riser is healthy, cheerful and industrious -French
The earth covers the errors of the physician -Italian
The earth does not belong to people, rather people to the earth -Native American
The earth is a beehive; we all enter by the same door but live in different cells
The earth is always frozen to lazy swine -Danish
*The Earth is round, go where thou wilt, to home thou art bound* -Swahili
The earthen pan gains nothing by contact with the copper pot -Danish
The earthen pot must keep clear of the brass kettle
The easiest way to double your money is to fold it in half and put it in your pocket -Country wisdom
The effect speaks, the tongue needs not

The effects of serious illnesses are often unknown -Latin
The egg should not try to teach the hen -Russian
The election of the abbot is not stopped for want of a monk -Italian
The elephant does not feel a flea-bite -Italian
The elephant does not get tired of its tusks -Masai
The elephant will reach to the roof of the house -Cameroonian
The elephant's head is no load for a child  –Sierra Leone
The Emperor of Germany is the king of kings, the King of Spain king of men, the King of France king of asses, the King of England king of devils -French
The Empires of the future are the Empires of the mind -Winston Churchill
The empty gives the way to the full -Arab
The end crowns all -Dutch
The end crowns the work
The end doesn't justify the means -Ovid
The end is only the beginning...
The end is the crown of any work -Russian
The end justifies/sanctifies the means
The end makes all equal
The end of mirth is the beginning of sorrow -Dutch
The end of one thing is only the beginning of another
The end of Passion is the beginning of Repentance - Ben Franklin
The end of the corsair is to drown -Italian
The end praises the work -Italian
The ending crowns the work
The ends justify the means -French
*The enemy has human needs and rational reasons heeds Panicking, he's drunk on fear help him deeper truths to hear* -Wampanoag
The enemy of my enemy is my friend -Arab
The enemy's cold heart summons the arrow to it -Zen
The energy it takes to run fast is wasted unless you know your destination
The envious man's face grows lean and his eye swells -Portuguese
*The errors of a wise man make your rule rather than the perfections of a fool* -William Blake
The essence of Zen is the absolute appreciation of all that was, absolute respect for all that is, and absolute love for all that is to be
The evening crowns the day
The everyday kindness of the back roads more than makes up for the acts of greed in the headlines -Charles Kuralt
The evil wound is cured but not the evil name
The evils we bring on ourselves are the hardest to bear
The excellency of hogs is-fatness; of men-virtue -Ben Franklin
The exception confirms/proves the rule -French

The exception proves the rule
The executive exists to make sensible exceptions to general rules
The existence of the sea means the existence of pirates -Malay
The experience of overcoming fear is extraordinarily delightful -Bertrand Arthur William Russell
The extreme law is the greatest injustice -Latin
The eye cannot rise above the eyebrow -Palestinian
The eye is bigger than the belly
The eye is blind if the mind is absent -Italian
The eye is the one that eats -Palestinian
The eye lets in love
The eye of a master does more work than both his hands -Palestinian, Slavic, Danish
The eye of the master fattens the horse -Italian, Spanish
The eye of the master makes the horse fat -Danish
The eye of the master makes the horse fat, and that of the mistress the chambers neat -Dutch
The eye sees, but the hand can't reach -Palestinian
The eye that sees all things else sees not itself
The eye will often wander the road that love has taught -Palestinian
The eyes are bigger than the belly -Dutch
The eyes are the window of the soul -English
The eyes believe themselves; the ears believe other people -German
The eyes of man speak words the tongue cannot pronounce -Crow
The eyes of others watch closely -Japanese
The eyes who don't see each other forget each other -Czech
The face is no index to the heart -English
The face is the index of the mind/heart
The fact that man knows right from wrong proves his intellectual superiority to other creatures; but the fact that he can do wrong proves his moral inferiority to any creature that cannot -Mark Twain
The fact that silence is golden may explain why there's so little of it
The fairest rose at last is withered
The falcon does not struggle when he is caught -Moroccan
The fall is nobody's sire -Kashmiri
The fall of a leaf is a whisper to the living - Danish, Russian
The falling out of lovers is the renewing of love
The false friend is like the shadow of a sun-dial -French
*The family that prays/plays together, stays together*
The farmers are the founders of civilization and prosperity
The farther from Rome, the nearer to God -Dutch
The farthest way about is the nearest way home
The fat is in the fire -John Heywood

The fat sow knows not what the hungry sow suffers -Danish
The fated will happen
The fault is great in proportion to him who commits it -French
The favourite finger gets the ring
The fear of ill exceeds the ills we fear
The fear of war is worse than war itself -Italian
The fearful are to be most feared
The fellow who blows his horn the loudest is generally in a fog
The fellow who never makes a mistake takes his orders from one who does
The few who do are the envy of the many who only watch - Jim Rohn
The fewer words, the better prayer -Martin Luther
The field is not plowed by turning it over in one's mind -Irish
The finest diamond must be cut
The fingers of the same hand are not alike -Portuguese
The fire burns brightest on one's own hearth -Danish
The fire heeds little whose cloak it burns -Danish
The fire is the test of gold; adversity of strong man
The fire is welcome within, when icicles hang without -Danish
The fire of adversity will melt you like butter, or temper you like steel. The choice is yours.
The fire which lights (or warms) us at a distance will burn us when near
The first [cup of vodka] goes as a stake, the second as a falcon, and the third as a little bird -Russian
The first at the mill grinds first -Italian
The first bird get the first grain -Danish
The first blow is as good as two -Italian
The first blow is half the battle
The first comer grinds first -French
The first dish pleases every one -Italian
The first drink with water, the second without water, the third like water -Spanish
The first duty of love is to listen
The first element of success is the determination to succeed
*The first faults are theirs that commit them, the second theirs that permit them*
*The first ill or mischief, seed  will a hundred others breed* -Italian
The first in the boat has the choice of oars -Dutch
*The first occasion offered quickly take, lest thou repine at what thou didst forsake* -Dutch
The first prerequisite of an advanced being is a sense of humor -Richard Bach
The first sign you are becoming spiritual is that you become cheerful

The first step binds one to the second -French
The first step is all the difficulty -French
The first step is as good as half over
The first step is the hardest
The first step is the only difficulty
The first step of handling anything is gaining an ability to face it
The first step to health is to know that we are sick
The first step to virtue is to abstain from vice
The first wealth is health
The fish always stinks from the head downwards -Russian
The fisherman fishes in troubled water -Portuguese
The flame is not far from the smoke -Danish
The flatterer's throat is an open sepulchre -Italian
The flawed pot lasts longest -French
The flimsier the product, the higher the price -Ferengi Rule of Acquisition
The flitch hangs never so high but a dog will look out for the bone -Danish
The flock follow the bell-wether
The fly flutters about the candle till at last it gets burnt -Dutch
The fly has her spleen and the ant her gall
The fly is small, but it is big enough to make one sick -Turkish
The fly on the water buffalo's back thinks he is taller than the water buffalo - Tagalog
The fly that bites the tortoise breaks its beak -Italian
The fly that plays too long in the candle, singes his wings at last
The flying hawk hides its talons -Native American
The fool cuts himself with his own knife -French
The fool does think he is wise, but the wise man knows himself to be a fool
The fool has his heart on his tongue, the wise man keeps his tongue in his heart
The fool hunts for misfortune -French
The fool is thirsty in the midst of water -Ethiopian
The fool knows more in his own house than the sage in other men's -Italian
The fool never undertakes little - Czech
The fool passes for wise if he is silent -Portuguese
The fool talks, and the wise man thinks
The fool thinks of the right way after the deed is done -Japanese
The fool who is silent passes for wise -French
The foot of the farmer manures the field -Danish
The foot of the owner is the best manure for his land -Danish
The forest can't be without its jackals -Azerbaijani
The forest has ears, and field has eyes -Danish

The forest is the poor man's overcoat  -New England
The forest will answer you in the way you call to it -Finnish
The formula for youth: Keep your enthusiasm and forget your birthdays
The fortress that parleys soon surrenders -Italian
The foundation of true joy is in the conscience
The fox advised the others to cut off their tails, because he had left his own in the trap -Italian
The fox changes his skin but not his habit
The fox does not go twice into the same trap -Danish
The fox goes through the corn and does not eat, but brushes it down with his tail -Galician
The fox knew too much, that's how he lost his tail
The fox knows much, but more he that catcheth him -Portuguese
The fox may grow grey, but never good
The fox may lose his hair, but not his cunning -Dutch
The fox never fares better than when he's banned -Dutch
The fox never found a better messenger than himself -Irish
The fox preys farthest from his home/den -Rumanian
The fox said the grapes were sour -Italian
The fox says of the mulberries when he cannot get at them; they are not good at all -French, from Aesop
The fox smells his own stink first
The fox that sleeps in the morning has not his tongue feathered -French
The fox thinks everybody eats poultry like himself -French
*The fox thrives best when he is most cursed* -French
The Fox's wiles will never enter the lion's head -French
The Frenchman sings well, when his throat is moistened -Portuguese
The friar preached against stealing and had a goose/pudding in his sleeve -Dutch
The friendship of great men is like the shadow of a bush, soon gone -French
The friendship of the great is fraternity with lions -Italian
The frog cannot out of her bog -Italian
The frog does not drink up the pond in which he lives –Nakota
The frog does not jump in the daytime without reason -Nigerian
The frog enjoys itself in water but not in hot water - Wolof
The frog in the well knows nothing of the great ocean
The frog likes water, but not boiling water -Senegalese
The frog wanted to be as big as the elephant, and burst -Ethiopian
*The frog will jump back into the pool, although it sits on a golden stool* -Dutch
The frost hurts not weeds -Dutch
The fruit falls not far from the stem -Dutch

The fruit of silence is tranquility -Arabic
The frying-pan said to the kettle, avaunt, black brows!
The fugitive finds everything impedes him -Italian
The full belly does not believe in hunger -Italian
The full cask makes no noise -Italian
The full person does not understand the needs of the hungry -Irish
The full-fed sheep is frightened at its own tail -Portuguese
The future belongs to him who knows how to wait
The future belongs to those who believe in the beauty of their dreams -
Eleanor Roosevelt
The future isn't what it used to be -Arthur C. Clarke
The future of society is in the hands of mothers; if the world was lost
through woman she alone can save it
The game is not worth the candle
The gardener had not yet dug out the radish, when the beggar held the
alms-bowl in front of him -Kashmiri
The gardener's dog does not eat lettuce and will not let others eat it
-Italian
The gardener's dog neither eats greens not lets any one else eat them
-Portuguese
The garment makes the man
The gem cannot be polished without friction, nor man perfected without
trials -Chinese
The generous man enriches himself by giving; the miser hoards himself
poor -Dutch
*The generous man grows rich in giving, the miser poor in taking* -Danish
The genius fails by his genius -Japanese
The gentle calf sucks all the cows -Portuguese
The gentle hawk mans herself -French
The Germans carry their wit in their fingers -French
The gift of happiness belongs to those who unwrap it
The girl who can't dance says the band can't play -Yiddish
The go-between wears out a thousand sandals -Japanese
The goat must browse where she is tied -Romanian
The goat which has many owners will be left to die in the sun -Haitian
The God/Creator gives us each a song –Ute
The gods send nuts to those who have no teeth
The gods too are fond of a joke -Aristotle
The golden age never was the present age -English
The golden key opens every door -Italian
The goldsmith, 100 blows, the blacksmith, one -Persian
The good cow gets sold in its own country -Maltese
The good die first: and those, whose hearts are dry as summer dust, burn

to the socket -Maltese
The good die young -Maltese
The good Lord didn't create anything without a purpose, but mosquitoes and sand gnats come close -Will Rogers
The good mother says not, "will you?" but gives -Portuguese
The good seaman is known in bad weather -Italian
The good shepherd shears, not flays -Italian
The good time comes but once -Italian
The good will of the governed will be starved if not fed by the good deeds of the governors -Ben Franklin
The good-looking boy may be just good in the face –Apache
The goose goes so often into the kitchen, till at last she sticks to the spit -Danish
The goose hisses, but does not bite -Dutch
The goose that has a good gander cackles loudly -Danish
The goose that has lost its head no longer cackles -Danish
The goslings would lead the geese out to grass -French
The gown does not make the friar/monk -Italian, French
*The gown is hers that wears it; and the world is his who enjoys it* -French
The grand instructor, time - Edmund Burke
The grandfathers and grandmothers are in the children; teach them well – Ojibwa
The grapes are sour
The grass is always greener in someone else's yard
The grass is always greener on the other side
The grass is always greener on the other side of the fence
The grass is greener on the other side
The grass is greener on the other side of the hill
The grass is greener on the other side, but it is just as hard to mow
*The grave may be dug very soon- with a knife, and fork, and spoon*
The great and the little have need one of another
The great fish eat up the small
The Great Spirit has a good side and bad side.  Sometimes the bad side gives us more knowledge than the good side. –Lakota
The great spirit is always angry with men who shed innocent blood –Iowa
The great thieves lead away the little thieves -French
The great, fantastic, magnificent truth is that the greatest of beauty waits, immanent, for your attention, and like a desert flower in rain, it blooms forth, when you notice it
The greater love is a mother's; then comes a dog's; then a sweetheart's -Polish
*The greater the fear the nearer the danger* -Danish
The greater the obstacle, the more glory in overcoming it

The greater the sinner, the greater the saint -English
The greater the truth, the greater the libel -English
The greatest barkers bite not sorest -English
The greatest burdens are not the gainfullest -French
The greatest cunning is to have none at all -French
The greatest evidence of demoralization is the respect paid to wealth -French
The greatest fool is he who worries about what he cannot help
The greatest friend of truth is time, her greatest enemy is prejudice, and her constant companion is humility
The greatest geniuses remain hidden -Plautus
The greatest good you can do for another is not just to share your riches, but to reveal to him his own -Benjamin Disraeli
The greatest hate springs from the greatest love -French, Slavic
The greatest honor history can bestow is that of peacemaker- Richard Nixon
The greatest king must at last go to bed with a shovel -French
The greatest liars talk most of themselves
The greatest mistake you can make in life is to be continually fearing you will make one
The greatest obstacle to progress is prejudice
The greatest of faults is to be conscious of none
The greatest pleasure I know is to do a good action by stealth, and to have it found out by accident - Charles Lamb
The greatest pleasure of life is love
The greatest remedy for anger is delay
The greatest step is that out of doors
The greatest strength is gentleness -Iroquois
The greatest talkers are always [the] least doers
The greatest things on earth have been done little by little -Thomas Guthrie
The greatest undeveloped territory in the world lies under your hat
The greatest wealth is contentment with a little
The green new broom sweepeth clean -John Heywood
The green twig is easily bent -Turkish
The greyhound that starts many hares kills none -Portuguese
The guests will go away, and we will eat the pasty -Portuguese
The habit does not make the monk[don't judge a book by its cover] -French, Portuguese
The habit of getting to the bottom of things usually lands a man on top
The half is better than the whole -Hesiod
The hammer shatters glass but forges steel -Russian
The hand that gives, gathers -Swedish

The hand that rocks the cradle, rules the world -William Ross Wallace
The hand with mud, the bread with honey -Albanian
The handsomest woman can only give what she has -French
The happiness of my/your life depends on the quality of my/your thoughts
The hardest person to awaken is the person already awake - Tagalog
The hardest step is that over the threshold -Italian
The hardest the problem is, the closer it is to be solved -Arabic
*The head and feet keep warm, the rest will take no harm*
The headache is mine and the cows are ours -Portuguese
The healthy die first -Italian
The heart at rest sees a feast in everything -Hindu
The heart does not lie -Dutch
The heart does not think all the mouth says -Italian
The heart leads whither it goes -French
*The heart must have its time of snow .. to rest in silence, and then to grow.*
The heart of the giver makes the gift dear and precious
The heart of the problem is a problem of the heart -Pam Mokler
The heart of the wise man lies quiet like limpid water -Cameroonian
*The heart sees better than the eye, hears better than the ear; knows that truth comes, bye and bye, illusion's veil is fear*
The heart sees further than the head
The heart that breaks open can contain the whole universe - Joanna Macy
The heart that loves is always young -Greek
The heart that once truly loves never forgets
The heart's letter is read in the eye
The heart's mirth does make the face fair
The heaviest thing I can carry is a grudge
The hen flies not far unless the cock flies with her -Danish
The hen is ill off when the egg teaches her how to cackle -Danish
The hen lives by pickings, as the lion by prey -Danish
The hen ought not to cackle in presence of the cock -French
The hen that stays at home picks up the crumbs -Portuguese
The hen's eyes are where her eggs are -Galician
The hen's eyes are with her chickens -French
The hen's eyes turn to where she has her eggs -Portuguese
The herb patience does not grow in every man's garden -Danish
The herb that can't be got is the one that heals -Irish
The hero appears only after the tiger is dead - Burmese
The heron blames the water because he cannot swim -Danish
The higher standing, the lower fall
The higher the monkey climbs, the more he shows his tail -John Wycliffe

*The higher the mountain the lower the vale, the taller the tree the harder the fall* -Dutch

The higher the mountain, the greater descent

The higher up, the greater the fall

The higher you climb, the heavier you fall -Vietnamese

The highest art is to conceal art

The highest tree hath the greatest fall

The hole is more honorable than the patch -Irish

The hole/calls invites the thief -Portuguese

The honest penny is better than the stolen dollar

The honey is sweet but the bee has a sting -Ben Franklin

The hood/habit/cowl does not make the monk

The horse may run quickly, but it can't escape its own tail -Russian

The horse must go to the manger, and not the manger to the horse -Danish

The horse one cannot have always has a fault -Danish

The horse that draws most is most whipped -French

The horse that pulls the most is whipped the hardest

*The horse that's hired, never tired*

The horse thinks one thing, and he that rides him another

The horse's best allowance is his master's eye -Portuguese

The hours of folly are measured by the clock, but of wisdom no clock can measure -William Blake

The hours that make us happy make us wise -John Masefield

*The house completed, possession defeated* -Italian

The house does not rest upon the ground, but upon a woman -Mexican

The house of the loud talker, leaks -Zulu

The house roof fights the rain, but he who is sheltered ignores it -Nigerian

The house shows the owner

The house sweeper's buttock is never at one direction -Nigerian

The house that is built after every man's advice seldom gets a roof -Swedish

The human tongue is more poisonous than a bee's sting -Vietnamese

The hunchback does not see his own hump, but he sees his brother's -French

The hungry belly has no ears

The hunter does not rub himself in oil and lie by the fire to sleep -Nigerian

The hunter in pursuit of an elephant does not stop to throw stones at birds -Ugandan

The hurrieder I go, the behinder I get Amish, German

The hurt man writes with steel on a marble stone

The husband is always the last to know -Ugandan, English

The hyena does not forget where it has hidden its kill -Thonga

The ideals and values of a nation are broadcast widely in its advertisements

The ignorant are obstructed by ignorance, while intellectuals are obstructed by intellectual knowledge -Muso Kokushi

The ignorant person is his own enemy -Arab

The ill year comes in swimming -French

The important thing in life is to have a great aim, and the determination to attain it

The important thing isn't how long you live, but how well you live -Seneca

The individual struggles and suffers for the well-being of the group -Native American

The infinite is in the finite of every instant -Zen

The injurer never forgets -Italian

The innkeeper loves the drunkard, but not for a son-in-law -Yiddish

The intemperate die young, and rarely enjoy old age

The interested friend is a swallow on the roof [preparing to head south for the Winter] -French

The Irish forgive their great men when they are safely buried -Irish

The is worthy of sweets, who has tasted bitters -Danish

*The issue of all contention is uncertain* [Witness the glorious uncertainty of the law, and of the turf -Danish]

The Italianised Englishman is a devil incarnate -Italian

The Italians are wise before the act, the Germans in the act, the French after the act -Italian

The Italians cry, the Germans bawl, and the French sing -French

The jay bird don't rob his own nest -West Indies

The journey is more important than the destination

The journey is the reward -Taoist

The journey of a thousand miles begins with a single step -Lao Tsu

The journey of a thousand miles begins with a single step, and continues step by step -Tao Te Ching

The joy of the heart makes the face fair/merry -Slavic

The just man may sin with an open chest of gold before him -Italian

The justification of profit is profit -Ferengi Rule of Acquisition

The kettle calls the pot black-brows (burnt-arse)

The kettle smuts the frying-pan -French

The key at the girdle keeps me good and my neighbour too -Portuguese

The key that is not used does not rust -Albanian

The kick of a mare never hurt a colt -Italian

The kick of the dam hurts not the colt

The kiln calls the oven burnt-hearth

The kind man feeds his cat before sitting down to dinner -Hebrew

The king is dead. long live the king!

The king of the bees has no sting -Portuguese
The king's cheese is half wasted in parings; but no matter, 'tis made of the people's milk - Ben Franklin
The laggard cow gets the sour grass -Danish
The lame goat does not take a siesta -Portuguese
The lame man runs if he has to -Norwegian
The lame tongue gets nothing
The language of truth is simplicity -Spanish
The last argument of kings [inscription of Louis XIV's cannon]
The last come is the best liked -French
The last comer shuts the door -Italian
The last comers are often the masters -French
The last drop maketh the cup run over -French
The last straw breaks the camel's back
The latecomers surpass the early starters
The later comer is ill lodged -Italian
The later you arrive at work, the earlier you can leave
*The law devised, its evasion contrived* -Portuguese
The law grows of sin, and chastises it
The law is good, if a man use it lawfully
The law of the strongest is always the best -French
The law says what the king pleases -French
The law, in its majestic equality, forbids the rich as well as the poor to sleep under bridges, to beg in the streets, and to steal bread -Anatole France
The lawyer's pouch is a mouth of hell -French
The lazy man is apt to be envious – Omaha
The lazy man who goes to borrow a spade says, "I hope I will not find one"  -Madagasy
The lazy man works more in the end -Czech
The lazy person must work twice - Latin American
The lazy pig does not eat ripe pears -Italian
The lazy servant takes eight steps to avoid one -Portuguese
The least said, the soonest mended/Least said, soonest mended
The leaves fall before the tree dies -French
The Lehua blossom unfolds when the rains tread on it -Hawaiian
The leopard does not change his spots -William Shakespeare
The less effort, the faster and more powerful you will be -Bruce Lee
The less hair a man has to comb, the more face he has to wash
*The less one thinks, the more one speaks* -French
The less said the sooner mended -Dutch
The less wit a man has, the less he knows that he wants it -Dutch
The less you know about an opportunity, the more attractive it is

The less you say, the more you don't have to apologize
The liar is not believed when he speaks the truth -Italian
The liar swears often by God -Arabic
The liar's punishment is not in the least that he is not believed, but that he cannot believe anyone else
The lie has short legs
The life of the wolf is the death of the lamb
The light heart lives long -Irish
The light is painful to sore eyes -Italian
The lion and the lamb shall lie down together, but the lamb won't get much sleep -Italian
The lion believes that everyone shares his state of mind - Mexican
The lion had need of the mouse -Italian
The lion is known by his claws -Italian
The lion is known by the scratch of his claws -Gaelic
The lion is not so fierce as he is painted
The lion's share
The list is worse than the cloth -French
The listener makes the backbiter -French
The little alms are the good alms -French
The lives of doctors, the souls of priests, and the property of lawyers, are in great danger -Italian
The lizard that jumped from the high iroko tree said he would praise himself if no one else did -Nigerian
The lone sheep is in danger of the wolf
The longer I live, the more convinced am I that this planet is used by other planets as a lunatic asylum –George Bernard Shaw
The longer the patient lives, the greater his chances of recovery
The longest day has an end
The longest journey begins with the first step, and continues, step by step by step -Tao Te Ching
The longest road out is the shortest road home -Irish
The longest way around is the shortest/nearest way home -Irish, Rumanian, Italian
The loquacity of fools is a lecture to the wise -Italian
The Lord takes care of drunks and sailors
The Lord will not fail to come, though he may not come on horseback -Danish
*The loss of wealth is loss of dirt, As sages in all times assert; The happy man's without a shirt* –John Heywood
The loss which your neighbour does not know is no real loss -Portuguese
The loudest bark rids not a dog of his fleas -Portuguese
The love of beauty is an essential part of all healthy human nature

The love of liberty is the love of others; the love of power is the love of ourselves - William Hazlitt

The love of money and the love of learning rarely meet

The love of money is the root of all evil

The love of wealth grows as the wealth itself grows -Latin

The loveliest of faces are to be seen by moonlight, when one sees half with the eye and half with the fancy -Persian

The low fig -fruit branch can be climbed by everyone -Albanian

The lowest fence is the easiest to get across -Norwegian

The lucky man has a daughter for his first-born -Portuguese

The mad dog bites its master -Portuguese

The magpie cannot leave her hopping -Dutch

*The main difference between men and boys is the price of their toys*

*The main thing is to keep the main thing the main thing*

The maintaining of one vice costs more than ten virtues

*The malady that is more incurable is folly -Portuguese*

The man has neither sense nor reason who leaves a young wife at home -French

The man of sense does not hang up his knowledge -Portuguese

The man of your own trade is your enemy -Portuguese

The man that creepeth, falleth not -Dutch

*The man who believes is the man who achieves*

The man who can't dance thinks the band is no good -Polish

The man who claims to be the boss in his own home will lie about other things as well –Amish

The man who does not learn is dark, like one walking in the night -Chinese

The man who does not love a horse cannot love a woman -Spanish

*The man who gives his opinion freely should be ready to fight fiercely –* Iowa

*The man who is afraid of asking is ashamed of learning -Danish*

The man who is born in a stable is not a horse -Danish

*The man who is scorned by women at twenty, chooses a younger one when he is forty*

The man who knows when not to act is wise. To my mind, bravery is forethought -Euripides

The man who lives only by hope will die with despair -Italian

The man who loves is easy of belief -Italian

The man who makes no mistakes does not usually make anything - Edward John Phelps

The man who never makes a mistake always takes orders from one who does -Italian

The man who rows the boat seldom has time to rock it -Bill Copeland

The man who spends his energies deliberately, has a great bank to draw on, and will draw the longest

The man who strikes first admits that his ideas have given out -Chinese

The man with the boots does not mind where he places his foot -Irish

The map is not the territory -Alfred Korzybski

The mare's kick does not harm the colt -Portuguese

The mare's kicks are caresses to the colt -Portuguese

The mark of shame does not wash away –Omaha

The mason who strikes often is better than the one who strikes too hard -Irish

The master derives from his art -Danish

The master of the people is their servant - Yemeni

The master orders the man, the man orders the cat, and the cat orders her tail -Portuguese

The master's eye and foot are the best manure for the field -Dutch

The master's eye makes the horse fat -Spanish

The master's footsteps fattens the soil, and his foot the ground

The maw costs much -Dutch

The maxims of men disclose their hearts -French

The mean is the best

The meaning is best known to the speaker -French

The meaning of a communication is the result you get -Richard Bandler

The meek shall inherit the earth. The rest of us will go to the stars.

The meeting of two personalities is like the contact of two chemical substances: if there is any reaction, both are transformed -Carl Jung

The memories of youth make for long, long thoughts -Lapp

The merchant that loses cannot laugh -French

The merchant who gains not, loseth -French

The middle way of measure is ever golden

The mighty oak tree was once a little nut that held its ground

The milk is spilled

The mill cannot grind with the water that is past

The mill does not grind without water -Italian

The miller is never so drunk that he forgets to take his dues -Danish

The miller sees not all the water that flows by his mill - Robert Burton

The mills of God grind slowly but they grind sure/finely -Irish

The mills of god grind slowly, yet they grind exceeding small

The millstone that lies undermost also helps to grind -Danish

The mind forgets, but the heart always remembers

The mind is for seeing, the heart is for hearing -Arabic

The mind is like a parachute, it's no good unless it's open

The mind is not a vessel to be filled but a fire to be kindled -Plutarch

The mind moves the matter -Latin

The mind, once expanded to the dimensions of larger ideas, never returns to its original size -Oliver Wendell Holmes -

The minute you settle for less than you deserve, you get even less than you settled for - Simone de Beauvoir

The miser and the pig are of no use till dead -French

*The miser fasts with greedy mind to spare; the glutton fasts to eat the greater share*

The miser is always in want

The miser's bag is never full -Danish

The mistakes are all waiting to be made -chessmaster Savielly Grigorievitch Tartakower [on the game's opening position]

The moment you wake, state your desire, picture your life as you desire it to be.  Minute to minute, throughout the day, nourish it, celebrate it, not wish, or anticipate, it's already here.  Celebrate it.

The money paid, the workman's arm is broken -French

The money the miser hoards will do him no good

The monk preached against stealing, and had the good in his larder -Dutch

The monk that begs for God's sake begs for two -French

The monkey knows the tree it climbs  –Puerto Riqueño

The moon does not heed the baying of dogs -Italian

The moon is a moon whether it shines or not

The moon is made of a green cheese -John Heywood

The moon is not seen where the sun shines

The moon is not shamed by the barking of dogs –Southwest Indian

The more a man exposes his nakedness the colder he is -French

The more a man knows, the less he knows he knows

The more a man knows, the more he is inclined to be modest

The more acquaintance, the more danger -English

The more adapted you are, the less adaptable you tend to be

The more by law, the less by right -Danish

The more cooks, the worse broth -Danish

The more corrupt the state is, the more numerous are the laws -Tacitus, *Annales*; Lao Tsu, *Tao Te Ching*

The more cost, the more honour -Slavic

The more fools, the more laughter -French

The more haste, the less speed -Slavic, French

The more I encourage a child to think for himself, the more he will care what I think

The more inches you give to someone, they more they become a ruler

The more knave, the better luck -Danish

The more noble, the more humble

The more one drinks, the more one may

The more riches a fool hath, the greater fool he is
The more servants, the worse service -Dutch
The more shepherds, the less care -Danish
The more shoots, the more leaves -Malay
The more sorrow one encounters, the more joy one can contain -Malay
The more the fox is cursed, the more prey he catches -Italian
The more the merrier -John Heywood
The more the well is used, the more water it gives/yields
The more things a man is ashamed of the more respectable he is
The more things change, the more they stay the same - Alphonse Karr
The more we do, the more we can do; the more busy we are, the more leisure we have
The more we overeat, the harder it gets to sit close to the table
The more we study, the more we discover our ignorance
The more wit, the less courage
The more women look in their glass, the less they look to their house
The more worked the steel is, the more beautiful it becomes -Albanian
The more you add, the worse it gets -Hebrew
The more you ask how far you have to go, the longer the journey seems – Seneca
The more you ask how much longer it will take, the longer the journey -Maori
The more you get, the more you want
The more you get, the wealthier you become. The more you give the richer your life becomes.
The more you give, the more good things come to you –Crow
The more you know, the less you need -Aborigine
The more you mow the lawn, the faster the grass grows -Albanian
The more you stir a turd, the worse it stinks -Romanian, Dutch
The more you stir filth the worse it stinks -Danish
The more you stir it, the more/worse it stinks -French
The more you stroke the cat's back the more she sets up her tail -Italian
The more, the merrier
The morning hour has gold in its mouth -German
The morning is wiser than the evening -Russian
The morning sun never lasts a day -Russian
*The morning to the mountain, the evening to the fountain*
The mortar always smells of garlic -Italian
The most beautiful sentiments in the world together weigh less than one action
The most covered fire is always the most glowing -French
The most cunning are the first caught -French
The most difficult mountain to cross is the threshold -Danish

The most exciting phrase to hear in science, the one that heralds new discoveries, is not Eureka! [I found it!] but That's funny - Isaac Asimov

The most exquisite folly is made of wisdom spun too fine -Ben Franklin

The most friendly fortune trips up your heels -French

The most important service rendered by the press is that of educating people to approach printed matter with distrust - Samuel Butler

The most important thing in communication is to hear what isn't being said

The most lasting monuments are doubtless paper-monuments -French

The most learned are not the wisest -Dutch

The most prudent yields to the strongest -Italian

The most solid friendships are often made in mutual adversity

The most useful learning in the world is that which teaches us how to die well

The most utterly lost of all days is that in which you have not once laughed

The most widespread form of compulsory education is experience

The moth does most mischief to the finest garment -Italian

The mother-in-law does not remember that she was once a daughter-in-law -Portuguese

The mother's heart is the child's schoolroom

The mountain has brought forth a mouse -Winston Churchill

The mountaineer's ass carries wine and drinks water -French

The mountains are in labour, and bring forth a mouse -Italian

The mountains shake, but do not fall -Albanian

The mouse in the wall may look at a cat, but he is wise not to squeak about it

The mouse is knowing, but the cat more knowing -Danish

The mouse may find a hole, be the room ever so full of cats -Danish

The mouse that has but one hole is soon caught -French

The mouse that hath but one hole is soon caught -Dutch, George Herbert

The Mouse that makes jest of a cat has already seen a hole nearby -Nigerian

The mouth of a wise man is in his heart; the heart of a fool is in his mouth

The mouth often utters that which the head must answer for -Danish

The mouth prays to Buddha but the heart is full of evil -Vietnamese

The mouth that says "Yes" can say "No"

The mud in Albania is sweeter than honey elsewhere -Albanian

The mud of one country is the medicine of another -Afghan

The mule long keeps a kick in reserve for its master -French

The Muses love the Morning - Ben Franklin

The myrtle is always a myrtle, though it be among nettles -Italian

The nail that sticks up will be hammered down -Japanese

The name is the omen -Latin
The nearer the bone, the sweeter the flesh -Portuguese, Dutch
The nearer the bone, the sweeter the meat -English
The nearer the church, the farther from God
The nearer the minster, the later to mass -French
The nearer to the church, the farther from God. -Polish
The nearer two beings or phenomena of like activity are to each other, the more they will repel each other. The farther away, the weaker the repulsion. All phenomena are ephemeral, constantly changing their constitution of yin and yang forces; yin changes into yang, yang changes into yin -1 of 12 theorems of the Unifying Principle, George Ohsawa
The nearest boor is the nearest kinsman when the calf lies in the ditch -Dutch
*The nest made, the bird dead* -Portuguese
The net of the sleeper catches fish -Greek
The new boat will find the old stones - Estonian
The new is always liked, though the old is often better -Danish
The next best thing to knowing a fact is knowing where to find it
The next message you need is right where you are -Baba Ram Dass
The nice thing about having nothing is that you don't have to worry about losing it
The niggard spends as much as he who is liberal, and in the end more -French
The night brings counsel -French
The night rinses what the day has soaped -Swiss
The nimblest footman is a false tale -French
The nobler the blood, the less the pride -Danish
The nobler the tree, the more pliant the twig -Dutch
The noblest dog can only bark -Dutch
The noblest vengeance is to forgive -Dutch,Portuguese
The noise is so great one cannot hear God thunder -French
The noisiest drum has nothing in it but air -English
The noisy fowler catches no birds -English
The north wind has no corn and a poor man no friend -English
The number one reason we forget is because we aren't paying attention in the first place - Lynn Stern
The object of war is not to die for your country but to make the other bastard die for his - General George Patton
The obstacle is the path
The offender never forgives -Russian
The oft-moved stone gathers no moss -Danish
The old branch breaks when it is bent -Danish
The old days will never be again, even as a man will never again be a

child –Dakota
The old dog doesn't bark for nothing
The old forget, the young don't know
The old goose plays not with foxes
The old horse leaves the load on the road -Albanian
The old law about an eye for an eye leaves everybody blind – Mahatma Ghandi
The old monkey gets the apple -French
The old one who is loved, is winter with flowers - German
The old ones sing, the young ones pipe -Dutch
The old ox plows a straight furrow -English
The old pipe gives the sweetest smoke -Irish
The old saints are forgotten in the new -Portuguese
The older one grows, the more one learns -Dutch
The older the fiddle the sweeter the tune -Irish
The older the fish, the louder the fishmonger yells.  The crummier the stock tip…
The older the goose, the harder to pluck
The one being carried does not realize how far away the town is -Nigerian
The one for the road should be a seat belt
The one great principle of English law is to make business for itself -Charles Dickens
The one thing worse than a quitter is the one who is afraid to begin
The one who cannot forget himself is easily forgotten by others
The one who draws a cart is urged on -Russian
The one who loves does not hate -Arab
The one who pulls a cart is urged on -Russian
The one who teaches is the giver of eyes - Tamil
The one who understands does not speak; the one who speaks does not understand - Chinese
The one without a sword will be humiliated -Arabic
The one-eyed are kings in the land of the blind -French
The one-eyed man does not thank God until he sees a blind man -Nigerian
The ones that matter most are the children.  They are the true human beings. –Lakota
The only absolute knowledge worth attaining is that your life is meaningless. My life? Well now, that's another story.. -Dr. Squid
The only cure for grief is action
The only difference between me and a madman is that I am not mad - Salvador Dali
The only normal people are the ones you don't know very well -Joe Ancis
The only people who are crazy enough to think they can change the world

are the people who do

The only real test in life is to conquer your fears

The only real voyage of discovery consists not in seeking new landscapes but in having new eyes -Marcel Proust

The only really good place to buy lumber is at a store, where the lumber has already been cut and attached together in the form of furniture, finished, and put inside boxes - Dave Barry

The only reason some people listen to reason is to gain time for rebuttal

The only secret a woman can keep is that of her age

The only thing necessary for the triumph of evil is for good men to do nothing -Edmund Burke

The only thing that men and women have in common, is that they both prefer the company of men -Oscar Wilde

The only thing that should surprise us is that there are still some things that can surprise us -Rochefoucauld

The only thing truth hurts is illusion

The only thing worse than being talked about is not being talked about -Oscar Wilde

The only thing worse than not getting what you want is getting what you want

The only thing worse than watching a bad movie is being in one -Elvis Presley

The only thing you control is your intention. That controls everything else.

The only time an average child is as good as gold is on April 1st

The only time you have too much fuel is when you're on fire -USAF

The only trouble with a sure thing is the uncertainty

The only truth is love. The only activity is service. The only peace is spiritual. The only satisfaction comes from doing all you can, where you are, with what you have, right now.

The only value of a collectible is what you can get somebody else to pay for it -Ferengi Rule of Acquisition

The only victory over love is flight -French

The only way out is through

The only way to get more than you give is to give more than you get

The only way to get rid of temptation is to give in to it - Oscar Wilde

The only way to get the best of an argument is to avoid it - Dale Carnegie

The only way to have a friend is to be one

The only way to keep a secret is to say nothing -French

The only wealth existing is understanding

The open door invites the thief -Dutch

The opera ain't over until the fat lady sings

The opportunity of a lifetime is seldom labeled so

The opposite of a correct statement is a false statement- but the opposite

of a profound truth may well be another profound truth -Niels Bohr
The optimist is as often wrong as the pessimist but is far happier
The outsider sees the best/most of the game
The oven must be at the proper temperature before you put the meat in it
-Country Wisdom
The owl does not praise the light, nor the wolf the dog -Danish
The owl thinks her children/own young the fairest -Danish
The ox that tossed me threw me into a good place -Portuguese
The pain of one is the pleasure of others [one man's meat is another
man's poison] -French
The pain of the little finger is felt by the whole body -Filipino
The pain of the mind is worse than the pain of the body
The palest ink is brighter/better than the best memory -Chinese
The pan says to the pot: Keep off, or you'll smutch me -Italian
The parson christens his own child first
The partridge loves peas, but not those that go into the pot with it -African
The passionate deny their anger, and cowards claim they know no fear
-Napoleon
The past is for wisdom, the present for action, but for joy the future
The past only exists if we re-create it in the present
The path down to evil is easy
The path is made by walking
The path of duty is the path of safety
The path to freedom is the return to your source
The path to glory is always rugged
The path to the rainbow is rain
The pathway to glory is rough, and many gloomy hours obscure it –Chief
Black Hawk
The patient may do without a doctor, but the doctor not without the patient
The peacock hath fair feathers, but foul feet -Slavic
The peasant will not cross himself before it begins to thunder -Russian
The pen is mightier than the sword
The pen is the tongue of the mind
The pencil of God has no eraser -Haitian
The people in the Land of the Eagle [North America] don't have to know
any more. They have more than enough books. They have the
knowledge. Now they simply have to live what they know. You have all
the information. You know it all. You are very mature people. You are
ready to fly. The only problem is that the knowledge is all in your minds. It
has to be transferred to your hearts -Don Alberto Tatzo, Yachag Shaman
The person afraid of bad luck will never know good -Russian
The person sins, then blames Satan for it -Afghan
The person who gets stuck on petty happiness, will not attain great

happiness -Tibetan
The person who has all the answers understands none of the problems
The person who has not traveled widely thinks his or her mother is the best cook -Ugandan
The person who is tired will find time to sleep -English
The person who knows everything has a lot to learn
The person who makes no mistakes usually does not make anything
The person who thinks too little talks too much
The person with burnt fingers asks for tongs -Samoan
*The petty thief will soon be jailed- the greater thief, the sooner hailed*
*The physician cures, nature heals*
The physician treats, nature cures -Latin
The pike grows big on small fry -Danish
The pine stays green in winter...Wisdom in hardship -Chinese
The pitcher goes often to the well and gets broken at last -French, Spanish, Dutch, Portuguese, English
The pitcher that goes often to the fountain leaves there either its handle or its spout -Italian, Portuguese
The pitcher will go to the well once too often -English
The place honors not the man; it is the man who honors the place -Hebrew
The pleasure of doing good is the only one that will not wear out -Chinese
The pleasures of the mighty are the tears of the poor
The plough gets not well if the ploughman hold it not
The plumber's house/roof always leaks -Turkish
The point of the thorn is small, but he who has felt it does not forget it -Italian
The poison of asps is under their lips -Italian
The poor are rich when they are satisfied
*The poor have little, Beggars none; The rich too much Enough not one* -Ben Franklin
The poor is hated by his neighbour, but the rich hath many friends -Italian
The poor lack much, but the greedy more -Swiss
The poor man eats at double cost -Portuguese
*The poor man fasting, has no meat; the rich man simply doesn't eat*
The poor man seeks for food, the rich man for appetite -Danish
The poor man seeks only a crumb, then finds he still hungers -Danish
The poor man wants much, the miser everything -Danish
The poor man's corm always grows thin -Danish
The poor writer blames the pen -Spanish
The pope and a peasant know more than the pope together -Italian
The post of honour is the post of danger
The pot boils best on your own hearth -Danish

The pot calling the kettle black
The pot calls the kettle black -Danish
The pot that boils too much loses its flavour -Portuguese
The pot upbraids the kettle that it is black -Dutch
The potter eats from a broken bowl
The power of accurate observation is frequently called cynicism by those who don't have it -George Bernard Shaw
The power of habit is great -Latin
The power of the wolf is in the pack -Native American
The praise of fools is censure in disguise -Dutch
The prayers of the wicked won't prevail -Rumanian
The price of a laugh is too high, if it is raised at the expense of another -Dutch
The price of greatness is responsibility
The price of liberty is eternal vigilance - U.S.A.F.
The price of your hat is not always the measure of your brain - African American
The pride of the poor does not endure -Danish
The priest errs at the altar -Italian
The priest to his book, the peasant to his plough -Danish
The proof is in the pudding -Miguel de Cervantes
The proof of the pudding is in the eating
The prudent embark when the sea is calm-the rash when the sea is stormy -Maori
The pumpkin gives birth and the fence has the trouble -Moroccan
The pure and simple truth is rarely pure and never simple -Oscar Wilde
The purest people are those with good manners -Arabic
The purpose of life is a life of purpose -Robert Byrne
The pursuit of happiness is the chase of a lifetime! It is never too late to become what I might have been
The quarrel of lovers is the renewal of love -Moroccan
The quickest way to do many things is to do only one thing at a time
The quickest way to double your money is to fold it and put it back in your pocket -Will Rogers
The quickest way to kill the human spirit is to ask someone to do mediocre work -Ayn Rand
The quieter you become, the more you can hear -Yasutani Roshi
The race is got by running
The race is not always to the swift but to those who keep on running
The race is not always to the swift, nor the battle to the strong [but that's the way to cast your bets]
The raggy colt often made a powerful horse -Irish
The rain can only drown the mud-rabbit if he hasn't the wits to keep his

mouth shut
The rain does not all fall on one roof
The rain falls on every roof -African
The rain falls on the just and unjust –Hopi
The rain follows after the forest -Hawaiian
The rainbow is a sign from Him who is in all things –Hopi
The rat does not leave the cat's house with a bellyful -Portuguese
The rat that knows but one hole is soon caught -Portuguese
The rattan basket criticizes the palm-leafed bag, yet both are full of holes
-Filipino
The raven always thinks that her young ones are the whitest -Danish
The raven chides blackness -Danish
The raven is fair when the rook is not by -Danish
The raven sees its chickens as falcons -Turkish
The real art of conversation is not only saying the right thing at the right
moment but also to leave unsaid the wrong thing at the most tempting
moment
The real leaders do not always march at the head of the procession
The real problem of one's leisure is to keep other people from using it
The real reason you can't take it with you is that it goes before you do
The reason many don't climb the ladder of success is that they're waiting
for the elevator
The reason we have time is so everything doesn't happen at once
The reason why worry kills more people than work is that more people
worry than work -Robert Frost
The reasons of the poor weigh not -Portuguese
The receiver is as bad as the thief
The recipe for success in business is often the same as for a nervous
breakdown
The relationship between truth and a newspaper is like the relationship
between the color green and the number seven. Occasionally you will see
the number seven written in green, but you learn not to expect this
-Garrison Keillor
The remedy against bad times is to have patience with them - Arabic
The remedy for injuries is not to remember them
The remedy is/may be worse than the disease
The remembrance of past sorrow is joyful
The reputation of a man is like his shadow; it sometimes follows and
sometimes precedes him, it is sometimes longer and sometimes shorter
than his natural size -French
The result validates the deeds -Latin
The reverse side also has a reverse side -Japanese
The reward of a thing well done, is to have done it -Emerson

The rich devour the poor, and the devil devours the rich and so both are devoured -Dutch
The rich don't fight - Japanese
The rich have many friends -Dutch
The rich have napkins, the poor have diapers
The rich man has his ice in the summer and the poor man gets his in the winter -Dutch
The rich man has more relations than he knows -French
The rich never have to seek out their relatives -Italian
The rich widow's tears soon dry -Danish
The rich worry over their money, the poor over their rice -Vietnamese
The rich would have to eat money if the poor did not provide food -Russian
The riches that are in the heart cannot be stolen -Russian
The richest man carries nothing away with him but a shroud -French
*The richest man, whatever his lot, is he who's content with what he has got* -Dutch
The richest soil, uncultivated, produces only weeds
The right answer to a fool is silence -Afghan
The right hand is slave to the left -Italian
The right man comes at the right time -Italian
The right place at the wrong time
The right time to dine is: for the rich man, when he is hungry; and for the poor, when he has something to eat -Mexican
The right to be heard does not automatically guarantee the right to be taken seriously -Hubert H. Humphrey
The right to swing my fist ends where the other man's nose begins - Oliver Wendell Holmes
The right-of-way is not something you have-somebody gives it to you
The righteous pays for the sinner -Portuguese
The ripest fruit will not fall into your mouth -Portuguese
The riskier the road, the greater the profit -Ferengi Rule of Acquisition
The river does not swell with clear water -Italian
The river passed the saint forgotten -Italian
The river past and God forgotten
The road to a friend's house is never long -Danish
The road to heaven is equally short, where'er we die -Danish
The road to hell is paved with good intentions -Samuel Johnson
The road to success is almost always under construction
The roaring lion kills no game -Tanzanian
*The robin and the wren are God's cock and hen; the martin and the swallow are God's mate and marrow*
The roots of a tree that grew up in the wind are strong - Japanese

The rose is red, yet its thorn is sharp
The roses fall, [and] the thorns remain -Italian
The rotten apple injures its neighbour -Italian
The Rotten apple spoils his companion -Ben Franklin
The rotten apple spoils the barrel -American
The ruin of a nation begins in the homes of its people -Twi [Ghana]
The ruling passion strong in death -Dutch
The Russian knows the way, yet he asks for directions -German
The sacrifice of time is the costliest of all sacrifices
The safest way to double your money is to fold it over and put it in your pocket -Kin Hubbard
The safety of a human is in the sweetness of his tongue -Arabic
*The Sages all this truth do know  Life doth ever onward flow*
The saint has no believers unless he works miracles -Italian
The saint who works no cures has few pilgrims to his shrine -French
The saint's-day over, farewell the saint -French
The salt of patience seasons everything - Italian
The same fire [which] purifies gold [and] consumes straw -Italian
The same hammer that breaks the glass forges the steel -Italian
The same night awaits us all -Horatius
The sap rises in the spring
The savage ox grows tame on strange ground -Portuguese
The scabbier the sheep the harder it bleats -Dutch
The scalded dog fears hot water, [and afterwards, cold] -Italian
The scar of the tongue is like the scar of the hand -Arabic
The school of experience charges high tuition, but fools learn nowhere else -Benjamin Franklin
The scoffer's own house is often on fire -Danish
The scraping hen will get something; the crouching hen nothing -Danish
The scythe ran into a stone -Russian
The sea complains it wants water
The sea has an enormous thirst and an insatiable appetite -French
The sea refuses no river -French
The seagull sees farthest who flies highest -French
The search for light and truth is never ending -Oriental
The second blow makes the fray -French
The second word makes the quarrel –Japanese
The secret of happiness is not doing what one likes to do, but in liking what one has to do -Sir James M. Barrie
The secret of life is honesty and fair dealing. If you can fake that, you've got it made -Groucho Marx
The secret of life is not to do what you like, but to like what you do -American

The secret of life is that there is no secret of life

The secret of seeing things as they are is to take off our colored spectacles. That being-as-it-is, with nothing extraordinary about it, nothing wonderful, is the great wonder. The ability to see things normally is no small thing; to be really normal is the unusual. In that normality begins to bubble up inspiration -Master Sessan

The secret of success in life is for a man to be ready for his opportunity when it comes

The secret of success is constancy of purpose

The secret of success is sincerity. Once you can fake that you've got it made -Daniel Schorr

The secret of success is your head up, your overhead down

The secret of two is God's secret, the secret of three is everybody's secret -French

The secret of wealth lieth in the letters SAVE

The seeds of the day are best planted in the first hour -Dutch

The seeker is the finder -Afghan

The seeking for one thing will find another -Irish

*The severity of the itch is inversely proportional to the reach*

The shadow of a lord is a cap for a fool -Italian

The shame you can't lift away, you had better let lie -Norwegian

The sharper the storm, the sooner it's over

The she-bear thinks her cubs pretty -Italian

The sheep on the mountain is higher than the bull on the plain -French

The sheep separated from the flock is eaten by the wolf -Turkish

The sheep that bleats the most give the least milk -Danish

The sheep that is too tame is sucked by too many lambs -French

The ship does not go without the boat -Italian

The shirt is nearer than the doublet -Italian

The shirt is nearer to the body than the coat -Danish

The shoe knows if the stocking has a hole - Bahamian

The shoemaker is barefoot and the carpenter's door is broken -Arabic

The shoemaker's child goes barefoot -Turkish

The shoemaker's children have no shoes

The shoemaker's son always goes barefoot -Danish

The shortest answer is doing [the thing]

The shortest distance between two points is how far apart they are

The shortest way to do many things is to do only one thing at a time

The shovel scouts the poker -French

The sick man is free to say all -Italian

The sick man sleeps when the debtor cannot -Italian

The sight of books removes sorrows from the heart - Moroccan

The sign invites you in, but your money redeems you out

The silence of the people is a warning for the king -French
The silent dog is the first to bite -German
The silent man is most trusted -Danish
The sinning is the best part of repentance -Arabic
The skill [of medicine] is long, the life [of patient and doctor] is short Ars longa, vita brevis -Hippocrates
The skillet can't call the pot black
The skin is nearer than the shirt -French
The sky is not the less blue because the blind man does not see it -Danish
The sky is wide, the earth is eternal –Japanese
The sky's the limit -Miguel de Cervantes
The sleeping fox catches no poultry -Danish
The sleeping Fox catches no poultry. Up! up!
The sleepy fox has seldom feathered breakfasts
The slothful man is the beggar's brother
The slow horse reaches the mill -Irish
The slower you go, the farther you will be -Russian
The sluggard will not plough by reason of the cold; therefore shall he beg in harvest, and have nothing -Russian
The small courtesies sweeten life; the greater ennoble it
The small sparkle often initiates a large flame -Latin
The smaller the waistline, the longer the life
The smallest good deed is better than the grandest intention
*The smallest thing outlives the human being* -Irish
The smart man learns more and more about how little he really knows
The smart one gives in -German
The smarter a man is, the more he needs God to protect him from thinking he knows everything –Pima
The smiles of a pretty woman are the tears of the purse
The smoke of a man's own house is better than the fire of another's
The smoke of my own house is better than another man's fire -Italian
The snake moves and erases its tracks -Albanian
The sneakiest two words in the English language are plus tax
The soldier is well paid for doing mischief -Italian
The soldier's blood exalts the captain -Italian
The solution to computer hardware problems: throw it away and buy a new one
The son like the mother, the daughter like the father -Chinese
The son-in-law's sack is never full -Portuguese
The song is very short because we understand so much -Navajo
The songbird sings because it has a song, not because it has answers Yet answers it has -Chinese

*The sooner begun, the sooner done* -Portuguese
The sooner you fall behind, the more time you'll have to catch up
The sooty oven mocks the black chimney -Portuguese
The soul is not where it lives, but it loves
The soul never thinks without a picture –Aristotle
The soul would have no rainbow if the eyes had no tears
The soul's joy is to expand to the Universal -Hawaiian
The sound of the bell does not drive away rooks -Italian
The sow prefers the mire -Danish
The Spaniard is a bad servant but a worse master -English
The spider and the fly can't make a bargain - Jamaican
The spirit in which we act nourishes or starves our spirit
The spirit is willing, but the flesh is weak
The spirit makes human beings noble -Latin
The squeaky wheel gets the grease [yet if it squeaks too much, it is replaced] -Ben Franklin
The stable wears out a horse more than the road -French
The standing precipice falls, the solid cliff breaks -Hawaiian
The stargazer's toe is often stubbed - Russian
The stars make no noise -Irish
The steed/horse does not retain its speed forever -Irish
The steps at court are slippery -Danish
The still sow eats up all the draft
The still swine eat the mash -Danish
The sting of a reproach is the truth of it -Ben Franklin
The stitch is lost unless the thread be knotted -Italian
The stone that everybody spits upon will be wet at the last -Danish
The stones of my river are as soft as a pillow -Tajik
The stranger is blind, be he even a seer -Arabic
The strength of the heart comes from the soundness of the faith - Arabic
The strength of the old is their ready counsel.
The strong should help the weak so that the lives of both shall be made easier -Aesop
The stronger the seam the worse the rent -French
The strongest is always in the right -Italian
The style is the man
The subconscious mind is a mental fireless cooker where ideas simmer and develop
The success of most things depends upon knowing how long it will take to succeed -Baron de Montesquieu
The sultan's sword is long -Arabic
The sun does not shine on both sides of the hedge at once
The sun doesn't shine on the same dogs back every day

The sun is still beautiful, though ready to set -Italian
The sun loses nothing by shining into a puddle -Italian
The sun passes over filth and is not defiled -Italian
The sun sets early for those who live always in the valley
The sun shines all alike
The sun shines even when it is cloudy -Albanian
The sun shines for all the world -French
The sun shines upon all alike -Latin
The sun will set without thy assistance -Hebrew
The sun will shine into our yard too
The superior person uses his mind like a mirror: it accepts all, it reflects all. It receives, but it does not keep -Chuang Tzu
The supreme law of the land is the Great Spirit's law, not man's law -Hopi
The supreme test of a person is his ability to make things go right
The surest way to be happy is to be busy
*The surest way to health, say what they will is to never suppose we shall be ill- most of the ills we mortals know from doctors and imagination flow*
The surest way to remain poor is to be an honest man -French
The sweetest grapes hang the highest
*The sweetest thing in life, is the welcome of a good wife*
The swindler readily cheats the covetous man -Portuguese
The sword and the ring according to the hand that bears them -Portuguese
The sword keeps the peace of the land -Danish
The tail does often catch the fox
The tail is always the hardest part to flay -Italian
The tail is the hardest to scourge -French
The tailor ill-dressed, the shoemaker ill-shod -Portuguese
The tailor makes the man
The tailor that makes not a knot loses a stitch
The talent of success is nothing more than doing well whatever you do without a thought of fame
The talkers sows, the listener reaps -Italian
The tallest blade of grass is the first to be cut by the scythe -Russian
The tallest tree is rooted in the ground -Russian
The Tao[way] is like a well: used but never used up. It is like the eternal void: filled with infinite possibilities. The Tao doesn't take sides; it gives birth to both good and evil. The great Tao flows everywhere. All things are born from it, yet it doesn't create them -Lao Tzu
The tar of my country is better than the honey of others -Moroccan
The task ahead of us is never as great as the Power behind us
*The tastiest fruit save for yourself, otherwise it sits on another's shelf –* Japanese

The teeth of the puppy are growing, while the old dog is gnawing bones -Danish

The teeth that laugh are also those that bite -Hausa

The Ten Commandments display was removed from the Alabama Supreme Court building. There was a good reason for the move. You can't post Thou Shalt Not Steal, Thou Shalt Not Commit Adultery and Thou Shall Not Lie in a building full of lawyers and politicians without creating a hostile work environment.

The ten thousand questions are one question. If you cut through the one question, then the ten thousand questions disappear -Zen

The tender surgeon makes the wound gangrene[Clean a wound out vigorously, at first, so it won't fester] -Italian

The thief becomes the gallows well -Portuguese

The thief does fear each bush an officer

The thief is frightened even by a mouse -Italian

The thief is no danger to the beggar -Irish

The thief is sorry he is to be hanged, not that he is a thief -Irish

The thief proceeds from a needle to gold, and from gold to the gallows -Portuguese

The thief thinks that all are like himself -Portuguese

The thief's wife does not always laugh -Italian

The third person makes good company -Dutch

The third time pays for all -Dutch

The thirteenth man brings death -Dutch

The thread breaks where it is weakest

The threatener sometimes gets a beating -French

The three foundations of learning: seeing much, suffering much, and studying much

The three things most difficult are, to keep a secret, to forget an injury, and to make good use of labour

The threshold of insult is in direct relation to intelligence

The tide tarrieth for no man -John Heywood

The tiger that has once tasted blood is never sated with the taste of it

The time is always ripe to do right -Nelson Mandela

The time is now, the iron's hot, do it quickly, late it's not

The time to relax is when you don't have time for it

The times are changed, and we are changed in them -Latin

The times change, and we change with them -John Owen

The time-travel convention will be held two weeks ago

The tired mare goes willingly to grass -Portuguese

The toe of the star-gazer is often stubbed -Russian

The tongue always returns to the sore tooth -Russian

The tongue ever turns to the aching tooth -English, Portuguese

The tongue has no bones, yet it breaks bones - Greek
The tongue is but three inches long, yet it can kill a man six feet high
The tongue is more to be feared than the sword -Japanese
The tongue is not steel, yet it cuts
The tongue like a sharp knife- Kills without drawing blood -Chinese
The tongue must be heavy, indeed, because so few people can hold it
The tongue of a person is the servant of his heart -Arabic
The tongue of idle persons is never idle
The tongue of the fool is the key to his death -Arabic
The tongue speaks, but the head doesn't know -Russian
The tongue talks at the head's cost
The tongue wounds more than a lance -French
The tooth often bites the tongue, and yet they keep together -Danish
The torch of doubt and chaos, this is what the sage steers by -Zen
The tortoise wins the race while the hare is sleeping
The tower in Pisa is straight- the rest of the world is crooked
The town that parleys is half surrendered -French
The trade of thick-headed Michael: eating, drinking, and idling -Dutch
The treason approved, the traitor abhorred -Portuguese
The tree can be recognized by its fruits -Latin
The tree is not felled at one blow -Italian
The tree is not to be judged of by its bark -Italian
The tree is sure to be pruned before it reaches the skies -Danish
The tree of liberty will not survive too much grafting
The tree will not sway without a trace of wind -Afghan
The Trojans were wise too late -Italian
The trouble with being a good sport is that you have to lose to prove it
The trouble with doing something right the first time is that nobody
appreciates how difficult it is
The trouble with love at first sight is second sight
The trouble with weather forecasting is that it's right too often for us to
ignore it and wrong too often for us to rely on it - Patrick Young
The true and the made are interchangeable. One can know with certainty
only what he have created himself -Latin
The true art of memory is the art of attention
The true test of a craftsman is how well he hides his mistakes
The true vocation of man is to find his way to himself -Hesse
The truest politeness comes from sincerity
The truly rich are those who enjoy what they have -Yiddish
The truth is not always what we want to hear -Yiddish
The truth stays like oil on water -Albanian
The truth will set you free -Latin
The truths we least like to hear are those which it is most to our

advantage to know

The turtle lays thousands of eggs without anyone knowing, but when the hen lays an egg, the whole country is informed -Malay

The two make a pair -French

The tyrant is only the slave turned inside out -Egyptian

The ugliest girl makes the best housewife

The unfortunate know who are their real friends -Italian

The unity of freedom has never relied on uniformity of opinion - John F. Kennedy

The universe rearranges itself to accommodate your picture of reality

The unknown does not tempt -Latin

The unknown is ever imagined -Greek

The unrighteous penny corrupts the righteous pound

The upright never grow rich in a hurry -Danish

The used key is always bright -Danish

The used plough shines, standing water stinks -Danish

The venom is in the tail -Italian

The victor will never be asked if he told the truth -Adolf Hitler

The vine brings forth three grapes: the first of pleasure, the second of drunkenness, the third of sorrow -Portuguese

The virtue of a man ought to be measured not by his extraordinary exertions, but by his everyday conduct

The virtue of parents is in itself a great legacy -Italian

The virtue of silence is a great piece of knowledge -Italian

The voice is the best music

The voice of one man is the voice of no one

The voice of the people is the voice of God -Roman

The wagon must go whither the horses draw it -Danish

The wallet of the timid man neither increases nor decreases -Maltese

The walls have ears -Arabic, Portuguese, Spanish

The watch-dog does not get sweet milk unless there be drowned mice in it -Danish

The watched pot doesn't boil/never boils

The water breaks out where it is not expected -Italian

*The water cuts through solid rock, w/persistence, gentle knock  Talent, Genius, Education; pale before Determination*

The water drop drills stone.  Endurance can overcome the obstacle even without the force.

The water is the same on both sides of the boat -Finnish

The water passes, the stones remain -Czech

The water runs while the miller sleeps -Danish

The water that bears the boat is the same that swallows it up

The water that does not flow is not fit to drink -Albanian

The way is made long through rules, but short and effective through examples -Latin

The way of the heart is love and joy

The way of the troublemaker is thorny –Umpqua

The way out is inward

The way to a man's heart is through his stomach -German

The way to learn is to begin

The way to overcome the angry man is with gentleness, the evil man with goodness, the miser with generosity and the liar with truth -Indian

The way to see by faith is to shut the eye of reason -Ben Franklin

The ways to the One are as many as the lives of men -Zen

The weak capitulates before the strong -Latin

The weakest go to the wall -Indian

The weakest must hold the candle -French

The weakness of the enemy makes our strength –Cherokee

The wealth of the mind is the only true wealth

The wearer best knows where the shoe pinches -Irish

The weather helps he who works -Albanian

The well fed does not understand the lean -Irish

The well-being of the patient is the most important law -Latin

The well-fed man does not believe in hunger -Italian

The wet branch burns better than the dry stone -Danish

The wheel of fate turns slow but it turns sure

The whisper of a pretty girl can be heard further than the roar of a lion -Arabic

The white coat does not make the miller -Italian

The whole hog or none -Italian

The whole ocean is made up of single drops -Italian

The whole principle is wrong; it's like demanding that grown men live on skim milk because the baby can't eat steak -Robert A. Heinlein, on censorship

The wicked even hate vice in others -Italian

The wicked flee when no man pursues them

The wicked shun the light as the devil does the cross -Dutch

The wife is the key of the house

The wife of a careless man is almost a widow -Hungarian

The wildcat does not make enemies by rash action.  He is observant, quiet, and tactful, and gains his ends. –Pawnee

The will is taken for the deed -French

The Will of God will never take you to where the Grace of God will not protect you

The wind cannot be caught in a net -Russian

The winds of heaven change suddenly; so do human fortunes

-Chinese
The windy day is not a day for scallops/thatching -Irish
The wine given to your workmen is that for which you get the best paid
-French
The wine in the bottle does not quench thirst
The wine is not known by the hoops -French
The wine-skin has its reasons for smelling of pitch -Portuguese
The wisdom of nations lies in their proverbs, which are brief and pithy
The wisdom of the wise and the experience of ages may be preserved by
quotation -Benjamin Disraeli
The wise adapt themselves to circumstances, as water molds itself to the
pitcher -Chinese
The wise and the brave dares own that he was wrong -Ben Franklin
The wise are instructed by reason; ordinary minds, by experience; the
stupid, by necessity; and brutes, by instinct
The wise do as much as they should, not as much as they can -French
*The wise for cure on exercise depend, God made no work for man to
mend*
The wise hand doth not all that the foolish mouth speaks
*The wise Indian this thing knows.. breathe not through mouth, but
through your nose.*
The wise man creates his destiny himself -Plautus
The wise man has long ears [big eyes] and a short tongue -German
The wise man hears the Tao[truth] and practices it diligently. The average
man hears of the Tao and moves on.  The fool hears of the Tao, and
laughs aloud.  If there were no laughter, the Tao would not be Tao -Lao
Tsu
The wise man is always a good listener
The wise man knows he knows nothing, but the fool thinks he knows it all
The wise man learns more from his enemies than the fool does from his
friends - Ben Franklin
The wise man never flies into a rage -Latin
The wise man sits on the hole in his carpet -Persian
The wise man's tongue is a shield, not a sword
The wise speak only of what they know
The wise through excess of wisdom is made a fool -Ralph Waldo
Emerson
The wise understand by themselves; fools follow the reports of others
-Tibetan
The wisest person knows he knows nothing -Socrates
The wish is [ever] father to the thought
The wit one wants spoils what one has -French
The witness of a rat is another rat -Ethiopian

The wolf and the dog agree, at the expense of the goat which together they eat -Basque

The wolf bemoans the sheep, and then eats it -Italian

The wolf eats of what is counted -Portuguese

The wolf feeds itself with its feet -Russian

The wolf has a thick neck because it has fast legs -Albanian

The wolf has a winning game when the shepherds quarrel

The wolf is always left out of the reckoning -Italian

The wolf is always said to be bigger than he is -Italian

The wolf is always said to be more terrible than he is -Italian

The wolf is never nearer than when we are talking of him

The wolf is not always a wolf -Italian

The wolf is not as big as people make him -French

The wolf is well pleased with the kick of a sheep -Portuguese

The wolf loses his teeth, but not his inclination -Portuguese, Spanish

The wolf may lose his teeth, but never his nature

The wolf never wants a pretext against the lamb -Portuguese

The wolf preys farthest from his home -Rumanian

The wolf preys not in his own field -Danish

The wolf taught us how to hunt -Cree

The wolf will die in his skin -French

The woman cries before the wedding and the man after -Polish

The woman who gives is seldom good; the woman who accepts is in the power of the giver -Italian

The woman who needs a man like a fish needs a bicycle soon finds that men prefer to be bicycles somewhere else

The wood is burnt, but the ashes are a nuisance -Afghan

The woods would be very silent if only the birds with the sweetest songs were heard

The word "Impossible" is not in my dictionary

The word of honour of a gentleman - another pledge would be better -French

The word of the old, and the gun of the young -Albanian

The word once spoken can never be recalled

The words are fair, said the wolf, but I will not come into the village -Dutch

The words fly away, the writings remain -Latin

The words of God are not like the oak leaf which dies and falls to the earth, but like the pine tree which stays green forever -Mohawk

The world to come is on its way- coming through us now, today

The work of the youth is the blanket of the old -Albanian

The work praises the man -Irish

The work shows the workman

The work will teach you - Estonian

The workman is known by his work
The workman is worthy of his hire -Dutch
The world belongs to early risers [the early bird gets the worm] -French
The world belongs to the phlegmatic -Italian
The world goes as men make it go; and men are free to make it go otherwise, if they have the courage
The world is a dangerous place to be not because of the people who do evil; but because of the people who stand by and let them - Albert Einstein
The world is a ladder for some to go up and others to go down
The world is a rose: smell it and pass it on to your friends  -Persian
The world is but a little place, after all
The world is comedy to those who think, a tragedy to those who feel
The world is divided into people who do things and people who get the credit. Try, if you can, to belong to the first class. There's far less competition - Dwight Morrow
The world is for him who has patience -Italian
The world is full of willing people: some willing to work and some willing to let them
The world is governed with little brains -Italian
The world is like a staircase; some go up, others go down -Italian
The world is sacred. You cannot improve it. If you try to change it, you will ruin it. If you try to hold it, you will lose it -Lao Tsu, *Tao Te Ching*
The world is the traveler's inn -Afghan
The world likes to be cheated -Dutch
The world owes you nothing-it was here first
The world wags on with three things: doing, undoing, and pretending -Italian
The world wants to be deceived, so let it be deceived! -Latin
The world would not make a racehorse of a donkey -Irish
The world's a stage; each plays his part, and takes his share -Dutch
The world's full of apathy, but I don't care
The worse service, the better luck -Dutch
The worse the carpenter, the more the chips -Dutch
The worse the passage, the more welcome the port -English
The worse the wheel, the more it creaks -Dutch
The worst ache is the present ache -Lebanese
The worst clothed go to windward -French
The worst emotion is envy -Arabic
The worst enemy you have is right in your head
The worst hog often gets the best pear
The worst jests are those that are true -French
The worst kind of enemies, are those who can praise -Tacitus

The worst men often give the best advice
The worst misfortunes are these that never happen
The worst pig eats the best acorn -Portuguese
The worst pig often gets the best pear -Italian
The worst prison is a closed heart -Pope John Paul II
The worst sinner has a future the greatest saint, past less than pure   No
one is as good or bad as they imagine, sure
*The worst sinner has a future; the greatest saint, past less than pure; no
one is as good or bad as they imagine, sure*
The worst use of success is to boast of it
The worst wheel always creaks most -French
The worst wheel creaks most -Italian
The worst wheel makes most noise -Dutch
The worst wheel of a cart creaks most -Romanian
The worst wheel of a cart makes the most noise - Ben Franklin
The worst whistlers whistle the most
The worth of a thing is best known by the want [of it] -Dutch
*The worth of a thing Is what it will bring* -Dutch, Portuguese
The wound of words is worse than the wound of swords -Arabic
The wrath of brothers is the wrath of devils -Portuguese
The wrong-doer never lacks excuses -Italian
The year has a wide mouth and a big belly -Danish
The years teach much which the days never know -Ralph Waldo
Emerson
The young cannot teach tradition to the old -Yoruba
The young cock crows as he hears the old one -Yoruba
The young have strength, the old have knowledge -Albanian
The young may die, the old must die -Dutch
The young pig grunts like the old sow
The young pig must often suffer for what the old sow did -Danish
The young ravens are beaked like the old -Dutch
Their dogs don't hunt in couples -French
*Their harms, our arms* -French
Them that have, gets
There are 3 kinds of men who don't understand women: young, old, and
middle-aged
There are a lot of judgmental people in the world, and I think all those
people are worthless dirtballs
There are as good fish in the sea as ever came out of it
There are bandits and there are bandits- sit on your wallet, and take care
with your heart
There are black sheep in every flock
There are but three ways of living: by working, by stealing, or by begging

There are fagots and fagots[all are not alike] -French
There are finer fish in the sea than have ever been caught -Irish
There are four kinds of people: those who make things happen, those who watch things happen, those who wonder what happened, and those who have absolutely no clue whatsoever
There are good and bad everywhere -Italian
There are good dogs of all sizes -French
There are ills that happen for good -Portuguese
There are lazy minds as well as lazy bodies -Ben Franklin
There are lees to every wine
There are many days in the year, and still more meals -Danish
There are many good moccasin tracks along the trail of a straight arrow – Fox
There are many more trap doors to failure than there are short cuts to success
There are many paths to profit -Ferengi Rule of Acquisition
There are many paths to the meaningful sense of the natural world
There are many paths to the top of the mountain, but the view is always the same -Chinese
There are many roads to Rome -Italian
There are many ways to the Creator –Arapaho
*There are more asses than carry sacks* -Italian
*There are more foolish buyers than foolish sellers* -French
There are more men threatened than stricken
There are more old drunkards than old doctors -Ben Franklin
There are more planes in the ocean than submarines in the sky -Navy
There are more thieves than are hanged -Dutch
There are more thieves than gibbets -Italian
There are more threatened than slain -Italian
There are more ways to the wood than one -Italian
There are no atheists in foxholes
There are no birds in last year's nest -Italian
There are no birds of this year in last year's nests
There are no children now-a-days -French
There are no degrees of honesty; either you are honest or you are not
There are no failures- only feedback -Richard Bandler
There are no foolish trades, there are only foolish people -French
There are no fools so troublesome as those that have wit -Ben Franklin
There are no free scholarships to the school of experience
*There are no gains without pains*
There are no great tasks in life- only small tasks done with great love -Mother Theresa
There are no impossible tasks to those with perseverance -Chinese

There are no incurable diseases- only incurable patients  –Dr. John Christopher

There are no mistakes, only lessons –Rule 3 of 10 Life Rules

There are no rules for success that work- unless you do

There are no secrets, and there is no mystery- There is only common sense –Onondaga

There are no sects in geometry -Voltaire [Francois-Marie Arouet]

There are no shortcuts to any place worth going -Beverly Sills

There are no small parts, only small actors

There are none so blind as they who will not see

There are none so deaf as they who will not hear

There are obviously two educations. One should teach us how to make a living and the other how to live.

There are old pilots, and bold pilots, but no old, bold pilots

There are only three kinds of people in the world: people who can count and people who can't

There are only two forces that unite men - fear and interest -Napoleon Bonaparte

There are only two powers in the world, the sword and the pen; and in the end the former is always conquered by the latter

There are only two types of Chinese- those who give bribes and those who take them -Russian

There are only two ways to live your life. One is as though nothing is a miracle. The other is as though everything is a miracle - Albert Einstein

There are some who despise pride with a greater pride -Italian

There are some who see ill, and would like to see worse -Italian

There are spots even on the sun

There are terrible temptations which it requires strength and courage to yield to - Oscar Wilde

There are those who can't see the forest for the trees -German

There are three bad neighbours: great rivers, great lords, and great roads -Danish

There are three enemies of personal peace: regret over yesterday's mistakes, anxiety over tomorrow's problems, and ingratitude for today's blessing

There are three faithful friends- an old wife, an old dog, and ready money -Ben Franklin

There are three kinds of lies: Lies, damned lies, and statistics -G.B. Shaw

There are three kinds of men: The ones that learn by reading. The few who learn by observation. The rest of them have to pee on the electric fence and find out for themselves -Will Rogers

There are three things from which no good can be got without a beating: a walnut-tree, a donkey, and a shrew -Danish

There are three ways of spreading news- telegraph, telephone, and tel-a-woman

There are too many chiefs and not enough Indians

There are toys for all ages -French

There are tricks in all trades -Italian

There are twenty-five uncaught sparrows for a penny -Afghan

There are two choices in life: Love and Fear.  Love is allowing what is. Fear is resisting it.

There are two great pleasures in gambling: that of winning and that of losing -French

There are two reasons for doing something: a really good reason and the real reason

There are two sides to every question

There are two sides to everything -German

There are two theories to arguing with a woman...neither works -Will Rogers

There are two ways to spread the light: to be the candle, or the mirror that reflects it -Edith Wharton

There can never be peace between nations until it is first known that true peace is within the souls of men –Oglala

There come as many calf-skins to market as ox-skins -Dutch

There die as many lambs as wethers -Portuguese

There goes more than one ass to market -Italian

There goes more to marriage than four bare legs in a bed -Italian

There has never been a great spirit without a touch of insanity -Latin

There is a 50 percent chance of anything- either it happens or it doesn't

There is a black sheep in every flock

There is a cause for all things -Italian

There is a core of good at the center of every human, no matter what the outside might look like. It can be reached with patient, caring persistence -Wampanoag

There is a crook in the lot of everyone

There is a fool at every feast -Dutch

There is a god inside us -Ovid

There is a great deal of difference between the eager man who wants to read a book, and the tired man who wants a book to read

There is a hole at the end of the thief's path –Lakota

There is a kind of pleasure in crying –Ovid

There is a limit to everything

There is a limit to one's patience

There is a measure in all things

*There is a pinch of the madman in every great man* -French

There is a remedy for all things save death -Dutch

There is a remedy for everything but death -Spanish
There is a scorpion under every stone
There is a skeleton in every house/the cupboard
There is a small choice in rotten apples
There is a sucker born every minute -P.T. Barnum
There is a time and place for everything
There is a time to be born, and a time to die
There is a time to let things happen and a time to make things happen
-Hugh Prather
There is a time to love, and a time to hate
There is a time to speak, and a time to be silent
There is a time to weep, and a time to laugh
There is always something higher –Japanese
There is another side to the picture
There is as good fish in the sea as ever came out of it
There is but one good mother-in-law and she is dead -English
There is but one step from the sublime to the ridiculous
There is great force hidden in a sweet command
There is great shame in forbidding something, and then doing it yourself
-Arabic
There is help for everything, except death -Danish
There is honor [even] among thieves -Danish, English
There is hope from the sea, but none from the grave -Irish
There is kindness to be found everywhere
There is life in the old dog yet
There is light at the end of the tunnel -Irish
There is little peace in that house where the hen crows and the cock is
mute -Italian
There is more hunger for love and appreciation in this world than for
bread -Mother Theresa
There is more than one fish in the sea
There is more than one way to skin a cat
There is more trouble in having nothing to do than in having much to do
There is much that cannot be understood by the poor soul that thinks
words are the same as thoughts
There is much to be said on both sides
There is neither wisdom nor courage in an empty belly
There is never a cry of "Wolf!" but the wolf is in the district -Italian
There is never any need to worry. We have enough shovels to bury
everybody.
There is never enmity between the cook and the butler -Italian
There is never enough where nought is left -Italian
There is never time to do it right, but there is always time to do it over

There is never wanting a dog to bark at you -Portuguese
There is no accounting for tastes
There is no appeal from time past -Italian
There is no avarice without penalty -Seneca
There is no beard so well shaven but another barber will find something more to shave from it -Italian
There is no beginning to practice  nor end to enlightenment; There is no beginning to enlightenment nor end to practice -Dogen
There is no bush so small but casts its shadow -French
There is no calamity greater than ignorance -Arabic
There is no chapel so small but has its saint -French
There is no companion like money
There is no cure against a slanderer's bite -Danish
There is no day without its night -Portuguese
There is no death, only a change of worlds –Duwamish
There is no dog, be he ever so wicked, but wags his tail -Italian
There is no end to learning
There is no enlightenment outside of daily life -Thich Nhat Hanh
There is no evil without good -Russian
There is no evil without something good -Latin
*There is no failure, only experience- give those who fail a second chance* -Wampaonoag
There is no fear where there is faith –Kiowa
There is no fire without smoke -Danish
There is no fireside like your own fireside -Irish
There is no first, without a second behind him -Arabic
There is no fishing for trout in dry breeches -Danish
There is no flavour in a swallowed morsel -French
There is no flying without wings -French
There is no fool like a learned fool -Italian
There is no fool like an old fool
There is no general rule without some exception
There is no getting blood from a turnip -Italian
There is no going to heaven in a sedan -Romanian
*There is no good accord where every man would be a lord*
There is no greater curse than total idleness
There is no hard bread if you are hungry -Spanish
There is no head so holy the devil doesn't make a nest in it
There is no helping him who will not be advised -Italian
There is no honor in poverty -Ferengi Rule of Acquisition
There is no hunting but with old hounds -French
*There is no jollity but hath a smack of folly*
*There is no joy without alloy* -Dutch

There is no law for fools
There is no liar lying like an angry man
There is no little enemy
There is no lock but a golden key will open it
There is no love without jealousy -Italian
There is no luck except where there is discipline -Irish
There is no making pancakes without breaking the eggs -Italian
There is no market for gloom. You cannot sell it. What the world wants, needs, and will buy is cheer.
There is no medicine against death
There is no need like the lack of a friend -Irish
There is no need to bind up one's head before it is broken -Italian
There is no need to blow what does not burn you -Danish
There is no need to fasten a bell to a fool, he is sure to tell his own tale -Danish
There is no paradise on earth equal to the union of love and innocence
There is no pillow so soft as a clear conscience -French
There is no place like home -French
There is no pleasure that does not pall, the more so if it costs nothing -Portuguese
There is no pot so bad but finds its cover -French
There is no pot so crooked that there isn't a lid to fit it
There is no pride like that of a beggar grown rich -French
There is no problem a good miracle can't solve
There is no reason to fly through a thunderstorm in peacetime -Sign over squadron ops desk, Davis-Monthan AFB, AZ, 1970
There is no right way to do a wrong thing -Turkish
There is no rose without a thorn
There is no royal road to learning
There is no rule without its exception
There is no second generation for a millionare -Japanese
There is no shame when you try and fail; there is only shame when you fail to try
There is no smoke without fire -French
There is no sovereignty like bachelorhood -Turkish
There is no spite like that of a proud beggar -French
There is no strength without unity -Irish
There is no substitute for brains, however silence can help
There is no substitute for success -Ferengi Rule of Acquisition
There is no such thing as a pretty good omelet -French
There is no such thing as an insignificant enemy -French
There is no teacher for love - Japanese
There is no thrill quite like doing something you didn't know you could

There is no time like the present
There is no use in blowing a fire that burns well -Danish
There is no use in saying, I will not go such a way, nor drink of such a water -Italian
There is no virtue in a promise unless it be kept -Danish
There is no warning for upcoming danger -Cheyenne
There is no way to happiness. Happiness is the way - Wayne Dyer, quoting Buddha
There is no wealth like unto knowledge, for thieves cannot steal it
There is no wool so white but a dyer can make it black
There is no worse fruit than that which never ripens -Italian
There is no worse robber/thief than a bad book -Italian
There is no worse water than still water -French
There is no worse water than that which sleeps -French
There is none so blind as those who will not see
There is none without a fault
There is no-one so rich he doesn't want more
There is not enough room for two elephants to sit in the same shade -African
There is not much danger that real talent or goodness will be overlooked long - Louisa May Alcott
*There is not so bad a gill, but there's as bad a will*
There is nothing either good or bad, but thinking makes it so
There is nothing hidden between Heaven and Earth -Venezuelan
There is nothing identical. Everything is unique. If one thing were totally like another, it would have to be that other. Everything is also becoming more unique, and individuating, or becoming more individual. 1 of 7 Universal Principles- George Ohsawa
There is nothing in this world constant but inconstancy
There is nothing lost by civility -Venezuelan
There is nothing neutral. There is always yin or yang in excess. No phenomena is balanced. Polarization is ceaselessly working and is universal. 1 of 12 theorems of the Unifying Principle, George Ohsawa
There is nothing new under the sun.
There is nothing so eloquent as a rattlesnake's tail –Navajo
There is nothing so secret but it transpires -Dutch
There is nothing so well done but may be mended -French
There is nothing stronger in the world than gentleness -Han Suyin
There is nothing that costs less than civility
There is nothing which has not been bitter before being ripe
There is nothing worse than apathy
There is one four-letter word you don't hear much any more-cash
There is one good thing you can give and still keep-your word

There is one who kisses, and the other who offers a cheek -French

There is only one nature - the division into science and engineering is a human imposition, not a natural one. Indeed, the division is a human failure; it reflects our limited capacity to comprehend the whole -Bill Wulf

There is only one pretty child in the world, and every mother has it -Chinese

There is plenty of corn in Castile, but he who has none, starves -Portuguese

There is plenty of sound in an empty barrel -Russian

There is reason in the roasting of eggs -Portuguese

There is safety in numbers

There is so much apathy in the world today .. but who cares?

*There is so much good in the worst of us, and so much bad in the rest of us, that it should remind all of us, not to criticize the rest of us*

There is some good in all of us; even a watch that won't run is right twice a day

There is something worse than growing old. It's the alternative.

There is something wrong with a person who is always right

There is strength in unity -German

There is the risk you cannot afford to take, -and there is the risk you cannot afford **not** to take -Peter Drucker

There is truth in wine

There is, to be sure, no evil without something good -Latin

There may be deep bottoms in still waters -Russian

There may be just one thing you don't know about a person, which if you did know, would completely change your opinion -Robert H. Lauren

There may be snow on the roof, but there's fire in the belly -Russian

There may be snow on the roof, but there's fire in the oven

There must be more to life than having everything! -Maurice Sendak

There never was a banquet so sumptuous but some one dined ill at it -French

There never was a looking-glass that told a woman she was ugly -French

There never was a scabby sheep in a flock that didn't like to have a comrade -Irish

There never was a shoe however handsome that did not become an ugly slipper -Italian

There never was an old slipper but there was an old stocking to match it -Irish

There was never a good war, or a bad peace -Benjamin Franklin

There were never fewer nobles than when all would be so -Danish

There will be trouble if the cobbler starts making pies -Russian

There will come a time when the seed will sprout -Russian

There will come a time when you believe everything is finished. That will

be the beginning.
There would be no great ones if there were no little ones -Slavic
There wouldn't be such a thing as counterfeit gold if there were no real gold somewhere -Sufi
There you go again
There's a sucker born every minute -P.T. Barnum
*There's many a slip between the cup and the lip*
There's no fool like an old fool
There's no need to fear the wind if your haystacks are tied down -Irish
There's no place like home
There's a difference between beauty and charm. A beautiful woman is one I notice. A charming woman is one who notices me -John Erskine
There's a difference between free speech and cheap talk
There's a difference between good sound reasons and reasons that sound good
There's a fine line between participation and mockery -Scott Adams
There's a great distance between word and deed -Spanish
There's a sucker born every minute; be sure you're the first to find each one -Ferengi Rule of Acquisition
There's always a calm before a storm
There's always a catch -Ferengi Rule of Acquisition
There's always a way out -Ferengi Rule of Acquisition
There's always an easy solution to every human problem -- neat, plausible, and wrong -Henry Louis Mencken
There's always room for improvement; It's the biggest room in the house
There's as good fish in the sea as ever came out of it
There's many a good cock come out of a tattered bag -English
There's many a good tune played on an old fiddle -English
There's many a knave concealed under a surplice -Danish
There's many a slip between the cup and the lip
There's many a slip 'twixt cup and lip -Danish
There's more knows Tom Fool than Tom Fool knows
There's neither rhyme nor reason -French
There's never a wise man without fault -Irish
There's no accounting for taste
There's no catching trouts with dry breeches -Portuguese
There's no compassion like the penny -Portuguese
There's no disputing about tastes -Italian
There's no fool like an old fool
There's no getting to heaven in a coach -Italian
There's no great loss without some gain -Italian
There's no guarding against the privy thief -French
There's no handsome woman on the wedding day, except the bride

-Portuguese
There's no harm in wine; it's drunkenness that is at fault -Russian
There's no hearth like your own hearth -Irish
There's no living without friends -Portuguese
There's no making a donkey drink against his will -Dutch
There's no making a silk purse of a sow's ear -Dutch
There's no making the ass drink when his is not thirsty -Italian
There's no meaning to a flower unless it blooms -Zen
There's no need to fear the wind if your haystacks are tied down -Irish
There's no need to grease the fat pig's rump -French
There's no shame in clothing you haven't cut yourself -Norwegian
There's no showing the wolf to a bad dog -French
There's no smoke with fire -Italian
There's no such thing as an unfair advantage -Ferengi Rule of Acquisition
There's no such thing as nonexistence
There's no thief like a bad book -Italian
There's no time like the present so just do it now, tomorrow may just
never come
There's no time like the present
There's no turning a windmill with a pair of bellows -Italian
There's none so blind as those who will not see   -Portuguese, Italian
There's none so deaf as those who will not hear
There's not enough if there's not too much -French
There's nothing like being bespattered for making a man defy the gutter
-French
There's nothing like change! -Cicero
There's nothing like having the key of the fields -French
There's nothing more dangerous than an honest businessman -Ferengi
Rule of Acquisition
There's nothing permanent except change -Greek
There's nothing wrong with charity...as long as it winds up in your pocket
-Ferengi Rule of Acquisition
There's plenty of room at the top, but there's no room to sit down
There's virtue in a man's face [presence carries weight] -French
These three are the marks of a Jew--a tender heart, self-respect, and
charity - Hebrew
These three take crooked ways: carts, boats, and musicians -Hindi
They - whoever they may be - can do whatever they want
They agree like cats and dogs -Dutch
They also serve who only stand and wait
They are as like as two peas in a pod
They are fools whose sheep run away twice -Dutch
They are never alone accompanied by noble thoughts

They are not dead who live in the hearts they leave behind –Tuscarora
They are rich who have friends -Portuguese
They assume most who know the least
They brag most of their ancestors who are unworthy of them -Danish
They bray most that [can] do least
They cackle often, but never lay an egg -Polish
They can because they think they can -Virgil
They can expect nothing but their labour for their pains -Cervantes
They die well that live well
They have most bread who have least teeth
They may forget what you said, but they will never forget how you made them feel
They must hunger in frost who will not work in heat
They need much whom nothing will content
They plan to fail who fail to plan
They planted so we ate, and we plant so they would eat  [People help others]  -Arabic
They say love is blind...and marriage is an institution. Well, I'm not ready for an institution just yet --Mae West
They say so is half a lie
They say, is a liar -Italian
They that/who live longest see most
They that be whole need not a physician, but they that are sick
They that can give up essential liberty to obtain a little temporary safety deserve neither liberty nor safety –Ben Franklin
They that have got good store of butter may lay it thick on their bread -Polish
*They that have no other meat, are glad to bread and butter eat*
They that live longest must die at last
They that marry in green, their sorrow is soon seen
They that sow in tears shall reap in joy
They that sow the wind shall reap the whirlwind
They understand one another like thieves in a fair -Dutch
They who are often at the looking-glass seldom spin -Dutch
They who cannot do as they would, must do as they can
They who come from afar have leave to lie -Dutch
They who do not wash well, do not bleach well -Danish
They who fight with golden weapons are pretty sure to prove their right -Dutch
They who give have all things; they who withhold have nothing -Hindi
*They who live in a worry- Invite death in a hurry*
They who love most are least valued -English
They who shun the smoke often fall into the fire -Italian

*They who sing through the summer must dance in the winter* -Italian
They will be hushed by a good deed who laugh at a wise speech -French
Thick wine is better than clear water -Italian
THIMK!
Things are not as they are, but as they are regarded -Italian
Things are to be tried - Japanese
Things at the worst will mend
Things done cannot be undone
*Things happen when you take action* -Japanese
Things past cannot be recalled
Things present are judged by things past
Things rashly taken end as ill
Things should be made as simple as possible, and not simpler -Albert Einstein
Things turn out best for the people who make the best of the way things turn out
Things turn up for the man who digs
Things unreasonable are never durable
Think about the misfortune of others that you may be satisfied with your own lot
Think all you speak, but speak not all you think
Think before you speak
Think first and speak afterwards
Think how happy you would be if you lost everything, then got it back again
Think in the morning. Act in the noon. Eat in the evening. Sleep in the night -William Blake
Think much, say little, write less -French, Italian
Think not on what you lack as much as on what you have -Greek
Think not that all truth is in your own school -Hawaiian
Think of ease, as you work on
Think of ease, but work on -English
Think of many things, do one -Portuguese
Think of the devil and he's looking over your shoulders
Think of your own faults the first part of the night, when you're awake, and the faults of others the latter part of the night, when you're asleep
Think on the end before you begin
Think today and speak tomorrow
Think twice before you do
Think win-win
Think with the wise but walk with the vulgar -German
*Think you can, or think you can't- and do you shall, or do you shan't*
Thinking good thoughts is not enough, doing good deeds is not enough,

seeing others follow your good examples is enough -Doug Horton

Thinking is not knowing -Portuguese

Thinking is one thing no one has placed a tax or tariff on

Thinking is the essence of wisdom -Persian

Thinking of where you are going, you forget whence you came -Portuguese

Thinking well is wise; planning well, wiser; doing well, wisest and best of all

Third time is the charm -Portuguese

Third time lucky -Portuguese

Third time pays for all -Portuguese

Thirst comes from drinking -Italian

Thirst is the end of drinking and sorrow is the end of drunkenness -Irish

This above all: to your own self be true, And it must follow, as the night the day, Thou canst not then be false to any man -Shakespeare

*This day is for me a gift- with it, universe will shift*

This horse is light in the mouth

*This the most important thing    feel good, allow your heart to sing*

This too will pass -German, Biblical

This world belongs to the energetic

This, too, shall pass -African

*Thistles and thorns prick sore, but evil tongues prick more* -Dutch

Thoroughly to teach another is the best way to learn for yourself

Those above are going down, those below are going up -Hawaiian

Those in a hurry do not arrive -Zen

Those needing proof refuse to see it -Walter Barton

Those that dislike cats will be carried to the cemetery in the rain -Dutch

Those that eat cherries with great persons shall have their eyes squirted out with the stones -Dutch, Portuguese

Those that lose wealth, lose much; those that lose friends, lose more; but those that lose spirit, lose all - Spanish

Those that make the best use of their time have none to spare

Those who are afraid of ghosts will find them -Arabic

Those who are feared are hated -Ben Franklin

Those who believe money can do everything are frequently prepared to do everything for money

Those who can, do. Those who can't, teach. Those who can't teach, teach teachers -G.B. Shaw

Those who can, do. Those who can't, criticize.

Those who climb high, often have a fall -Danish

Those who complain most are most to be complained of

Those who dislike cats will be carried to the cemetery in the rain -Dutch

Those who eat best and drink best often do worst

*Those who eat most are not always fattest; those who read most, not always wisest*

Those who fail to plan, plan to fail

Those who fight dragons become dragons

Those who fight fire with fire burn their houses down twice as fast -Vietnamese

Those who have free seats at a play hiss first -Chinese

Those who have one food in the canoe and one in the boat will fall in the river –Tuscarora

*Those who ignore warnings plain- will soon pay a price in pain*

*Those who in quarrels interpose, must often wipe a bloody nose* - Ben Franklin

Those who live amongst wolves must learn to howl like wolves -Russian

Those who live in glass houses should not throw stones

Those who lose dreaming are lost -Aborigine

Those who make peaceful revolution impossible will make violent revolution inevitable -John F. Kennedy

Those who say it is impossible need to get out of the way of those doing it -Chinese

Those who sleep with dogs will rise with fleas -Italian

Those who stand for nothing fall for anything -Alex Hamilton

*Those who suck at the glass tit- [television] find their minds are as empty as it* -Native America

Those who work deserve to eat; those who do not work deserve to starve

Those who would give up essential liberty to gain temporary safety deserve neither

Thou art a bitter bird, said the raven to the starling

Thou shalt not practice mirth control

Thou too art mortal –Latin

Though a lie be swift, truth overtakes it -Italian

Though a lie be well dressed, it is ever overcome

Though a tree grow ever so high, the falling leaves return to the ground -Malay

Though honey is sweet, do not lick it off a briar -Irish

Though I am not naturally honest, I am so sometimes by chance -William Shakespeare

Though malice may darken truth, it cannot put it out

Though old and wise, yet still advise

Though one should conquer a million men on the battlefield, yet he, indeed, is the noblest victor who has conquered himself -Dhammapada

Though the ass may carry a sack of gold, it nevertheless feeds on thistles -Danish

Though the bamboo forest is dense, water flows through it freely -Zen

Though the bird may fly over your head, let it not make its nest in your hair -Danish
*Though the bird's in the net It may get away yet* -Danish
Though the carpenter is bad, the splinter is good -Irish
Though the fool waits, the day does not -French
Though the fox runs, the pullets/chickens have wings -Italian
Though the heavens fall, there will be a hole to escape through
Though the heron flew high, the falcon kills it -Portuguese
Though the mastiff be gentle, yet bite him not by the lip -Portuguese
Though the wound be healed, yet a scar remains
Though thee hath never so many counsellors, yet do not forsake the counsel of thy own soul
Though thine enemy seem a mouse, yet watch him like a lion
Though we may pluck flowers by the way we may not sleep among flowers -Portuguese
Though you cast out nature with a fork, it will still return -Portuguese
Though you teach a wolf the paternoster, he will say "Lamb! Lamb!"
*Though your enemy is the size of an ant, regard him as an elephant* -Danish
Though your mastiff be gentle, do not bite his lip -Portuguese
Thought breaks the heart -Cameroonian
Thought he was a great catch, turns out he is a shackle -Arabic
Thought is free -Cameroonian
Thought is the seed of action
Thoughts are like arrows- released, they strike their mark.  Guide them well, or one day you may be your own target. –Navajo [Dineh Nation]
Thoughts are male, words are female -Italian
Thoughts are things[yet unborn in form]
Thoughts be free from toll
*Thoughts held in mind- produce after their kind*
*Thoughts become words, and words become deeds; deeds become habit, from which character bleeds*
Threads do not break for being fine, but for being gouty and ill-spun -Portuguese
Threatened folks eat bread -Portuguese
Threats are arms for the threatened -Italian
Threats don't kill -Dutch
Three brothers, three castles -Italian
Three brothers, three fortresses -Portuguese
Three diseases without shame: Love, itch and thirst -Irish
Three feet of ice does not result from one day of cold weather -Chinese
Three good meals a day is bad living -Ben Franklin
Three know it, all know it -Italian

Three makes a company -Latin
Three may keep a secret, if two of them are dead -Italian
Three may keep counsel if two be away
Three moves equal a fire -Benjamin Franklin
Three or four daily will bring you to the bottom of the sack -Portuguese
Three removes are as bad as a fire
Three Spaniards, four opinions -Spanish
Three things cannot long be hidden the sun, the moon, and the truth
-Confucius
Three things drive a man out of doors: smoke, dropping water, and a
shrew -Italian
Three things drive a man out of his house - smoke, rain and a scolding
wife
Three things it is best to avoid: a strange dog, a flood, and a man who
thinks he is wise -Welsh
*Three things must epigrams, like bees, have all- a sting, and honey, and
a body small* -Latin
Three things reborn each day; the echo of the woods, the rainbow, and
woman's beauty
Three ways there are to learn wisdom: by reflection, which is noblest;
imitation, which is easiest; and by experience, which is bitterest -
Confucius
Three women and a goose make a market -Polish
Thrift is better than an annuity -French
Thrift is good revenue
Thrift is truly a virtue- especially in an ancestor
Thrive by honesty or remain poor -French
Through being too knowing the fox lost his tail -Italian
Through difficulty, sweetness -Latin
Through hardship to the stars
Through obedience learn to command
*Through this toilsome world, alas! Once and only once I pass; If a
kindness I may show, If a good deed I may do To a suffering fellow man,
Let me do it while I can. No delay, for it is plain I shall not pass this way
again.*
Through unity the small thing grows, through disunity the largest thing
crumbles -Latin
Throw a lucky man into the sea and he will come up with a fish in his
mouth -Arabic
Throw away the apple because of the core
Throw good to your left and right, and you'll find it when you'll need it
-Czech
Throw no stones at a sleeping dog -Danish

Throw not the child out with the bath -Danish
Throw not thy hatchet at the Lord, He will turn the sharp edge against thee -Danish
Throw out a sprat to catch a mackerel/salmon/herring/whale
Throw out the rule book. Rules = fear and fear = rules. Be fully present.
Throw that bone to another dog -Portuguese
Throw your sadness to God, not to your  fellow human being -Swahili
Throwing your cap at a bird is not the way to catch it -Portuguese
Thrust not thy finger in a fool's mouth -Dutch
Thundershowers and great men's favour are always partial -Danish
Thus fareth the world, that one goeth up and another goeth down
Thy friend has a friend, and thy friend's friend has a friend, so be discreet
Tie me hand and foot and throw me among my own people -Italian
Tied to the sour apple-tree -Italian
Tim was so learned, that he could name a horse in nine Languages - Ben Franklin
Time and opportunity are no man's slave
Time and place make the thief -Dutch
Time and straw make medlars ripe -Dutch
Time and the hour are not to be tied with a rope -Portuguese
Time and tide wait for no man
Time and words can never be recalled
Time brings roses -Dutch
Time cures all things
Time destroys all things -Dutch
Time devours all things
Time discloses/reveals all things
Time does not bow to you, you must bow to time
*Time fleeth away without delay* -Dutch
Time flies, but remember: you are the navigator
Time flies -Latin
*Time gained, much gained* -Dutch
Time gives good advice -Maltese
Time goes, death comes -Dutch
Time has wings
Time heals old pain, while it creates new ones -Hebrew
Time is a good/great story teller -Irish
Time is a great healer -Hebrew
Time is an inaudible file -Italian
Time is God's and ours -Dutch
Time is like a sword. If you do not cut it, it will cut you -Arabic
Time is like the ocean, always there, always different -Ogden Nash
Time is money, but money is not time

Time is money -Dutch, German
Time is nature's way of keeping/preventing everything from happening at once
Time is not tied to a post, like a horse to the manger -Danish
Time is the father of truth
Time is what keeps everything from happening at once
Time lost cannot be won again
Time marches on
Time past cannot be called back again
Time past never returns, a moment lost, lost for ever
Time past never returns -Dutch
Time reveals all things
Time shall teach thee all things
Time spent in getting even would be better spent in getting ahead
Time tames the strongest grief
Time teaches all things, heals all wounds, and wounds all heels
Time tries all
Time tries truth
Time waits for no man -Danish
Time will tell -Danish
Time works great changes
Time works wonders -Danish
Time, as he grows old, teaches many lessons
Times change and we with them
Times passes like the wind -Portuguese
Timid dogs bark most
Timing has a lot to do with the outcome of a rain dance -Country Wisdom
Tired folks are quarrelsome -French
'Tis a fat bird that bastes itself -Dutch
'Tis a good farthing that saves a penny -French
'Tis a good horse that has no fault -French
'Tis a hard winter when one wolf eats another -Russian
'Tis a long day a day without bread -French
'Tis a silly sheep that confesses to the wolf -Italian
'Tis a silly sheep that makes the wolf her confessor -French
'Tis a sorry ass that will not bear his own burden
'Tis a wise child that knows its own father -Dutch
'Tis altogether vain to learn wisdom, and yet live foolishly -Dutch
'Tis as necessary to him as gold weights are to a beggar -Dutch
'Tis best woo where a man can see the smoke -Dutch
'Tis better to have loved and lost, than never to have loved at all -Dutch
'Tis day still, while the sun shines -Dutch
*'Tis easy to see, hard to foresee* - Ben Franklin

'Tis everywhere the same as here -French
'Tis good feasting in other men's houses -Italian
'Tis hard to hold a conger by the tail -Gaelic
'Tis possible if true -French
'Tis sweet at certain times to drop the sage -French
'Tis the great art of life to manage well the restless mind
'Tis the last straw that breaks the camel's back -French
*'Tis too late to spare when the cask is bare -Dutch*
*'Tis true now, 'twas true of old- best travel companion is silver and gold*
'Tis well that wicked cows have short horns -Dutch
Tit for tat is fair play
*Tithers do not poorhouse see- nor do they e'er know poverty*
*Tithers you will never see- begging, or in poverty*
To a bad worker, no good tools -French
*To a boiling pot flies come not*
To a bold man fortune holds out her hand -French
To a crazy ship every wind is contrary -Italian
To a friend's house the road is never long -Danish
*To a good cat, a good rat -French*
To a hasty question a leisurely answer -Portuguese
To a mind that is still, the whole universe surrenders -Chuang-tzu
To a quick question give a slow answer -Italian
To a rogue, a rogue and a half -French
To a young heart everything is sport -Italian
To accept a favour is to sell freedom -Latin
To accomplish many things, do them one at a time
To acquire knowledge, one must study; but to acquire wisdom, one must observe
To acquire wealth is difficult, to preserve it more difficult, but to spend it wisely most difficult of all
To act is easy, to think, hard
To act sincerely with the insincere is dangerous -Taoist
To affirm that every person has inherent worth and dignity is an understatement as great as saying that Bill Gates has some money
To alcohol! The cause of - and solution to - all of life's problems! -Homer Simpson
*To all you that aid you, more than rote- always send a thank you note*
*To any fine cat, a fine rat -French*
To any smart guy, someone smarter by one half -French
To ask the hard question is simple -W. H. Auden
To attract good fortune, spend a new coin on an old friend, share an old pleasure with a new friend, and lift up the heart of a true friend by writing his name on the wings of a dragon -Chinese

To avoid that run-down feeling, cross the streets carefully

To bait and to grease does not retard a journey -Danish

To be a fool at the right time is also an art -Danish

To be angry with a weak man is a proof that you are not very strong yourself

To be free is not merely to cast off one's chains, but to live in a way that respects and enhances the freedom of others -Nelson Mandela

To be good is to be happy

To be loved is to be fortunate, but to be hated is to achieve distinction

To be loved, love! -Latin

To be of use in the world is the only way to be happy

To be prepared for war is one of the most effectual means of preserving peace

To be proud of virtue, is to poison yourself with the Antidote -Ben Franklin

To be rich is not everything, but it certainly helps -Yiddish

To be slow in giving and to refuse, are alike -Portuguese

To be successful, learn what you do best, then do it

To be suspicious is to invite treachery

To be virtuous is to do good

To be what we are, and to become what we are capable of, is the only end in life

To be willing is to be able -French

To become rich in this world, it needs only to turn one's back on God -Italian

To believe a thing impossible is to make it so -French

To bend a bamboo, start when it is a shoot -Malay

To care for wisdom and truth and the improvement of the soul is far better than to seek money, honour and reputation

To censure princes is perilous, and to praise them is lying -Italian

To change and change for the better are two different things -German

To change one's habits smacks of death -Portuguese

To circumstances and custom the law must yield -Danish

To compare is not to prove -French

To cut into another man's ear is like cutting into a felt hat -Danish

To deceive a diplomat speak the truth, he has no experience with it -Greek

To deny all, is to confess all -Spanish

To do like the monkey, get the chestnuts out of the fire with the cat's paw -French

To do nothing teacheth to do evil -Dutch

To do, one must be doing -French

To each his own

To each life a purpose -Arabic

To eat and drink, and sleep together, is marriage, methinks -French
To enjoy life we must touch much of it lightly -Voltaire
To err is human, but when the eraser wears out ahead of the pencil, you're overdoing it
To err is human, to blame the next guy even more so
To err is human, to forgive, divine
To err is human, to persist devilish -Latin
To err is human, to repent divine; to persist devilish -Ben Franklin
To every bird its nest seems fair -French
To every fool his cap -Dutch
To every lord every honour -French
To every saint his candle -French
To every saint his torch -Italian
To expect what never comes, to lie in bed and not sleep, to serve well and not be advanced, are three things to die of -Italian
To fail to do good is as bad as doing harm -Plutarch
To fall out of the frying-pan into the fire -Italian
To fear love is to fear life, and those who fear life are already three parts dead -Bertrand Russell
To follow the path, look to the master, follow the master, walk with the master, see through the master, become the master -Zen
To forgive is to set the prisoner free and then discover the prisoner was you
To forgive our enemies is a charming way of revenge
To forgive the blood- as in a killing- is to be a man -Albanian
To frighten a bird is not the way to catch her -Slavic
To gain a good reputation, endeavor to be what you desire to appear -Socrates
To gain teaches how to spend
To get eggs there must be some cackling -Dutch
To get the chicks one must coax the hen -French
To give counsel to a fool is like throwing water on a goose -Danish
*To give is honour, to beg is dishonour* -Portuguese
To give tardily is to refuse -French
*To give you must be willing to receive. To receive you must be willing to give.*
To go as fast as a friar that is invited to dinner -French
To go on a vision quest is to go into the the presence of the great mystery -Lakota
To go safely through the world you must have the eye of a falcon, the ear of an ass, the face of an ape, the mouth of a pig, the shoulders of a camel, and the legs of a deer -Italian
To God's council-chamber there is no key -Danish

To gossip is like playing checkers with an evil spirit- you win occasionally, but are more often trapped at your own game –Hopi

To grow rich one has only to turn his back on God -French

To handle yourself, use your head. To handle others, use your heart.

To hang your sickle on another man's corn -Dutch

To have "Heard say" is half a lie -Italian

To have a stomach and lack meat; to have meat and lack a stomach; to lie in bed and cannot rest; are great miseries

To have a true friend, you must be a true friend

To have eye one on the cat and another on the frying-pan -Italian

To have luck needs little wit -Italian

To have money is a fear, not to have it a grief

To hear a hundred times is not so good as to see once

To him that does everything in its proper time, one day is worth three

*To him who can take what thou hast, give what he asks* -Italian

To him who gives you a pig you may well give a rasher -Italian

To him who is determined it remains only to act -Italian

To him who watches, everything reveals itself -Italian

To know a man well, one must have eaten a bushel of salt with him -French

To know all is to forgive all -French

To know and not do is the same as not knowing

To know and to act are one and the same -Samurai

To know everything is to know nothing -Italian

To know how country folks are doing, look at their barns, not their houses

To know how to wait is the great secret of success

To know oneself is true progress

To know the disease is half the cure

To know the law and do the right are two things -Danish

To know the road ahead, ask those coming back -Chinese

To know which way the wind blows, put your wet thumb in the air.  But if you do it too often, your thumb will get moldy.

To lather an ass's head is only wasting soap -Portuguese

To laugh often and much; to win the respect of intelligent people and the affection of children; to earn the appreciation of honest critics and endure the betrayal of false friends; to appreciate beauty; to find the best in others; to leave the world a bit better, whether by a healthy child, a garden path, or a redeemed social condition; to know even one life breathes easier because you have lived: this is to have succeeded -Ralph Waldo Emerson

To learn obeying is the fundamental art of governing

To leave a place is to die a little -French

To lend is to buy a quarrel -Indian

To live a creative life, we must lose our fear of being wrong -Joseph Chilton Pearce

To live in the hearts of those left behind is not to die

To live is not all of life, nor death to die

To live long is almost everyone's wish, but to live well is the ambition of a few

To live long is to suffer long -Danish

To lose a friend is the greatest of all loses

To love and be loved is to feel the sun from both sides -David Viscott

To love and be wise is incompatible -Portuguese

To love and to be loved is the greatest happiness of existence

To love and to be wise are two different things -French

To love is to choose -French

To love something is to give it room enough to grow

To love your enemies is fine, so treat your friends even better

To make a happy couple, the husband must be deaf and the wife blind -French

To make a success of old age you must start young

To make enemies, talk; to make friends, listen

To make peace is more daring, more creative, and more enduring than to make war -Karen Armstrong

To make the cart go you must grease the wheels -Italian

To marry a woman for her beauty is like buying a house for its paint

To marry one is a duty; twice a folly; thrice is madness -Dutch

To mention the wolf's name is to see the same

To one who has a pie in the oven, you may give a bit of your cake -French

To preserve a friend three things are required: to honour him present, praise him absent, and assist him in his necessities

To preserve friendship one must build walls -Italian

To promise and give nothing is comfort for a fool -Italian

To promise is easy, to keep is troublesome -Danish

To promise much means giving little -Portuguese

To protest and knock one's head against the wall is what everybody can do -Italian

To read without reflection is like eating without digestion

To really understand a man we must judge him in misfortune

To rebel in season is not to rebel -Greek

To refuse praise is to seek praise twice

To reprove a fool is but lost labour -French

To rise at five, dine at nine, sup at five, go to bed at nine, makes a man live to ninety-nine -French

To rise at six, eat at ten, sup at six, go to bed at ten, makes a man live

years ten times ten -French
To rob a robber is not robbing -French
To rude words, deaf ears -French
To rule the mountains is to rule the river -French
To run away is not glorious, but very healthy -Russian
To save time is to lengthen life
To say little and perform much is the characteristic of great minds
To say nothing, especially when speaking, is half the art of diplomacy
-Will Durant
To scare a bird is not the way to catch it -French
To see a just cause and not to act is the act of a coward -Japanese
To see it rain is better than to be in it -French
*To see what few have seen- go where few have been* -Buddha
To see what is in front of one's nose needs a constant struggle -George
Orwell
To set up what you like against what you don't like- this is the disease of
the mind -Sayen Shaku
To squeeze an eel too hard is the way to lose it -French
To steal ideas from one person is plagiarism; to steal from many is
research
To strive, to seek, to find, and not to yield
To succeed in the world it is not enough to be stupid, you must also be
well-mannered -Voltaire [Francois-Marie Arouet]
To talk goodness is not good. Only to do it is -Chinese
*To talk without thinking is to shoot without aiming*
To teach is to learn -Japanese
To the ass, or the sow, their own offspring appears the fairest in creation
-Latin
*To the bold man, Fortune holds out her hand* -Portuguese
To the devil with so many masters, said the toad to the harrow -French
To the fallen tree, hatchets! hatchets!
*To the grave a pall, and that's all*
To the jaundiced all things seem yellow -French
To the lean pig, a fat acorn -Portuguese
To the man behave like a man, to the dog behave like a dog -Albanian
To the mediocre, mediocrity appears great -Indian
To the mind that is still, the whole universe surrenders -Taoist ideal
*To the pure, all is pure* -Latin
To the Raven, her own chick is white -Irish
To the world, you may be one person, but to one person, you may be the
world
To touch the earth is to have harmony with nature –Oglala
To travel hopefully is a better thing than to arrive, and the true success is

to labour

To truly know a thing, one must live it completely, in the body, for then the heart knows it also -Amazon Indian

To wait and be patient soothes many a pang -Danish

To want the same in intentions and disinclinations is what makes a firm friendship -Sallustius

To want to forget something is to remember it -French

To wash an ass's head is but loss of time and soap -French

To what shall I compare this life of ours? Even before I can say it is like a lightning flash or a dewdrop it is no more -Sengai

To whom do you offer your shells for sale? To people who come from Saint Michel [where shells abound] -French

To whom God gives, to him also the people give -Polish

To whom you tell your secret you surrender your freedom -Italian

To whom you tell your secrets, to him you resign your liberty -Spanish

To withhold truth is to bury gold -Danish

To work is to pray -Latin

To worry about tomorrow is to be unhappy today

To youth I have but words of counsel - work, work, work

Toast the mochi but not your hand - Japanese

Today a man, tomorrow none

Today for money, to-morrow for nothing -Dutch

Today gold, tomorrow dust

Today in gold, to-morrow in the mould -Danish

Today is practice for tomorrow

Today is that tomorrow you thought about yesterday

Today is the first day of the rest of your life - North American Saying

Today is the scholar of yesterday

Today is the tomorrow you worried about yesterday -Dale Carnegie

Today is yesterday's pupil

Today me, tomorrow you -Maltese

*Today red, to-morrow dead* -Dutch

*Today stately and brave, to-morrow in the grave* -Dutch

Today you; tomorrow me -Maltese

*Today, enjoys his halls, built to his mind, tomorrow, in a coffin is confined*

Today, make an investment in someone else's happiness

Today's mighty oak is yesterday's nut that held its ground

Today's deeds make tomorrow's history

*Today's sorrow brings nought to-morrow* -Dutch

Together we stick, divided we are stuck

Tom Thriftless buys what he doesn't want because it is a bargain

Tomorrow comes never

Tomorrow is a new day -English

Tomorrow is another day
Tomorrow is often the busiest day of the week -Spanish
Tomorrow never comes/Some-a-day never comes/Some-a-day I'm a goin' to do this
*Tongue breaks bone and herself has none*
Too err is human -Dutch
Too far East is West -English
Too full of courtesy, full of craft -Franklin
Too hot to last -English
Too keen an edge does not cut, too fine a point does not pierce -French
Too late the bird cries out when it is caught -French
Too late to grieve when the chance is past -French
Too little and too much spoils everything -Danish
Too little, too late -Danish
Too many captains will sink the ship -Danish
Too many cooks oversalt the porridge -Dutch
Too many cooks spoil the broth -German
Too many folks go through life running from something that isn't after them
Too many jokes bursts out the pus -Swahili
Too many of us conduct our lives on the cafeteria basis-self-service only
Too many of us don't care what happens so long as it doesn't happen to us
Too many parents are not on spanking terms with their children [parody of speaking]
Too many square meals make too many round people
Too much ain't enough
Too much attention to little things leaves too little time for the big things
Too much breaks the bag
Too much familiarity breeds contempt -Portuguese
Too much honey cloys the stomach -Slavic
Too much humility brings humiliation -Arabic
Too much humility is pride
Too much knowledge makes the head bald -Russian
Too much laughter discovers folly
Too much liberty spoils all
Too much of a good thing is wonderful -Mae West
*Too much of one thing is good for nothing* -Dutch
Too much praise is a burden
Too much scratching smarts, too much talking harms -French
Too much spoils, too little is nothing
Too much water drowned the miller -French
Too much wax burns the church -Portuguese

Too much zeal spoils all -French
Too swift arrives as tardy as too slow
Too to will in two -French
Touch not another man's money, for the most honest never added to it -French
Touch pitch, and you will be defiled
Touch the hole in your life, and there flowers will bloom -Zen
Tough times don't last but tough people do -French
Tracers work both ways -U.S. Army Ordnance
Trade follows the flag -French
Trade is the mother of money -Polish
*Trade knows neither friends or kindred* -French
Traffic increases to fill the road space available
*Translators, traitors* -Italian
Travel broadens the mind -Italian
*Travel east or travel west, a man's own home is still the best*
Travelers from afar can lie with impunity -French
Treachery and slander are long lived -Danish
Treachery darkens the chain of friendship, but truth makes it brighter than ever –Conestoga
Treachery lurks in honeyed words -Danish
Treachery returns -Irish
Treachery will come home to the traitor
Tread on a worm and it will turn -French
Treat people in your debt like family, exploit them ruthlessly -Ferengi Rule of Acquisition
Trickery comes back to its master -French
Trim my beard, and I will trim your top-knot -French
Trouble follows sin as surely as fever follows chill –Hopi
Trouble is merely opportunity dressed in work clothes
Trouble no man about his religion- respect his views, and expect respect for yours –Shawnee
Trouble rides a fast horse  -Italian
Trouble shared is trouble halved-joy shared is joy doubled -German
Trouble with a milk cow is she won't stay milked
Troubles never come singly
True blue will never stain
True charity is not a luxury.  It's the seed corn for your own good.
True coral needs no painter's brush
True friendship is a plant of slow growth
True friendship is like sound health, the value of it is seldom known until it be lost
True friendship lasts forever

True jokes never please -French
True joy is a serious thing –Seneca
True love decreases the pain of poverty
True love is giving, not taking
True love never dies -German
True love never grows old -Italian
True love never runs smoothly
True love shows itself in time of need
True nobility is in being superior to your previous self -Hindustani
True nobility is invulnerable -French
True praise roots and spreads
*True wisdom is know what is best worth knowing, and to do what is best worth doing*
*Truly is that one a friend- Who never speaks words to offend*
Trumpet in a herd of elephants; crow in the company of cocks; bleat in a flock of goats -Malayan
Trust a dishonest man as far as you can throw him
Trust, but take care whom -Latin
Trust everybody, but cut the cards yourself -W.C.Fields
Trust everybody, but thyself most -Danish
Trust in Allah, but tie your camel -Arab
Trust in God but lock your doors -Russian
Trust in God, but take care of your garden
Trust is the biggest liability of all -Ferengi Rule of Acquisition
Trust is the mother of deceit
Trust me, but look to thyself -Irish
Trust not a dog that limps -Portuguese
Trust not a horse's heel, nor a dog's tooth
Trust not a horse's heels -Portuguese
Trust not a new friend or an old enemy -Portuguese
Trust not a skittish horse, nor a great lord, when they shake their heads -Danish
Trust not much in a new friend or an old house
Trust not still water nor a silent man -Danish
Trust not the praise of a friend, nor the contempt of an enemy
Trust not to God but upon good security -French
Trust not tow with firebrands, nor a woman with men -Portuguese
Trust thyself only, and another shall not betray thee
Trust was a good man; Trust-not was a better -Italian
Trust your own instinct. Your mistakes might as well be your own, instead of someone else's -Billy Wilder
Truth always prevails. Live in honesty and truth, for that is like medicine, it will take care of you, no matter the externals -Cree

Truth and folly dwell in the wine-cask -Danish
*Truth and love are two of the most powerful things in the world; and when they both go together they cannot easily be withstood*
Truth and oil always come to the surface -Spanish, Portuguese
Truth and oil are ever above
Truth and roses have thorns about them
Truth comes out of the mouths of babes -French
Truth does not happen, it just is –Hopi
Truth fears no trial
Truth fears not the flames of slander and injustice
Truth finds foes, where it makes none
Truth has a handsome countenance but torn garments -German
Truth has a scratched face
Truth hath a good face, but ill clothes
Truth is bitter food -Danish
Truth is God's daughter -Danish
*Truth is honest, truth is sure; Truth is strong and must endure*
Truth is mighty and will prevail
Truth is owned by everyone
Truth is stranger than fiction
Truth is the best advocate
Truth is the club that knocks down and kills everybody -French
Truth is the daughter of time
Truth is the foundation of all knowledge, and the cement of all societies
Truth is the opinion that survives
Truth is the safest lie -Jewish
Truth is time's daughter
Truth lies at the bottom of a well
Truth lies at the bottom of the decanter
*Truth may be blamed, but cannot/shall never be shamed*
*Truth may be both scarce and bland- yet supply exceeds demand*
Truth may be suppressed, but not strangled -German
Truth must be seasoned to make it palatable -Danish
Truth needs no colour; beauty, no pencil
Truth needs not many words
Truth never grows old
Truth never perishes -Seneca
Truth stands the test of time; lies are soon exposed   Bible -Proverbs 12:19
Truth will be out -Latin
Truth will conquer
Truth will out
Truth will prevail

Truth will stand without a prop
Truth, once crushed, will rise again
Truth's best ornament is nakedness
Truth's cloak is often lined with lies -Danish
Try [your friend] before you trust him
Try to look unimportant; they may be low on ammo -Infantry Journal
Try to see yourself as others do- but try not to get mad about it
*Trying is lying; trying is dying.  Do, or don't do* -Alan Cohen
Turn over a new leaf
Turn your face to the sun and the shadows fall behind you -Maori
Turn your tongue over in your mouth seven times before talking [think before you speak] -French
Twigs can be rectified if corrected[Knowledge is best gained young] -Arabic
*'Twixt the cup and the lip there's many a slip* -French
'Twixt the word and the deed there's a long step -French
Two are the masters of one -Danish
Two bigs will not go in one bag -Portuguese
Two blacks do not make a white -Slavic
Two can live as cheap[ly] as one, if one doesn't eat
Two can play [at] the game
*Two cats and a mouse, two wives in one house, two dogs and a bone, never agree in one*
Two cocks in one yard do not agree -Italian
Two dogs fight for a bone and a third runs away with it -Italian
Two dogs over one bone seldom agree
Two dogs strive for a bone, and a third runs away with it
*Two dogs to one bone, may never accord in one*
Two ears to one tongue, therefore hear twice as much as you speak
Two eyes see more than one -Portuguese
Two heads are better than one –John Heywood
*Two in distress makes sorrow less*
Two is company, but three is none
Two is company, three's a crowd
Two may keep counsel if one be away
Two may lie so as to hang a third -Danish
*Two men looked out through prison bars- one saw mud, the other, stars*
Two men may meet, but never two mountains -French
Two of a kind make a pair
Two of a kind, whate'er they be -French
Two of a trade seldom agree
Two persons cannot long be friends if they cannot forgive each other's little failings

Two quarrel and a third profits by it
Two shorten the road -Irish
Two Sir Positives can scarce meet without a skirmish -Irish
Two small antelopes can beat a big one -Twi, Ghana
Two sparrows on one ear of corn make an ill agreement -Portuguese
Two sparrows on the same ear of corn are not long friends -French
Two sparrows upon one ear of corn make ill agreement -French
Two swords do not fit in one sheath [Two masters rarely agree] -Arabic
*Two things prolong your life: A quiet heart and a loving wife*
Two thirds of the work is the semblance -Irish
Two to one is odds -Irish
Two watermelons can't be held in one hand -Afghan
Two women and a goose make a market -Italian
Two wrongs do not make a right -English
*Two wrongs don't make a right, but they often make a fight*
Two's company, three's a crowd
Two-thirds of help is to give courage -Irish
*Two-thirds of promotion is motion*
*Unbending the bow does not cure/heal the wound -Italian*
Uncertainty rules, from cradle to the grave
Under a pear tree, never fix the hat - Japanese
Under a ragged coat lies wisdom -Romanian
Under a ragged coat may lie wisdom
Under a shabby cloak may be a smart drinker -Portuguese
Under a tattered cloak you will generally find a good drinker -Spanish
Under fair words beware of fraud -Portuguese
Under his bowl there is a little bowl -Afghan
Under the sackcloth there is something else -Portuguese
Under white ashes lie often glowing embers -Danish
Under white ashes there is glowing coal -Italian
*Undeserved praise sometimes reacts as poison in disguise*
Uneasy lies the head that wears a crown
*Uneducated son? No shame- for the father is to blame -Chinese*
Unhappiness is not knowing what we want and killing ourselves to get
Union is strength -French
Union makes strength -Portuguese
Unite to move forward -Hawaiian
United we stand; divided we fall -Aesop
Unity is strength
University politics are vicious precisely because the stakes are so small - Henry Kissinger
Unjustly got wealth is snow sprinkled with hot water -Chinese
Unkindness destroys love

Unless hell is full no lawyer will ever be saved -French
Unless you can create the WHOLE universe in 5 days, then perhaps giving advice to God isn't such a good idea!
Unless you enter the tiger's den you cannot take the cubs -Japanese
Unless you try to do something beyond what you've already mastered,you will never grow
Unless your opponent is much inferior, do not attack until he has been disorganized and demoralized –Sun Tzu
Unpleasant advice is a good medicine
Unpolished pearls do not shine
Unprofitable eloquence is like the cypress, which is great and tall, but bears no fruit
Unstringing the bow does not cure the wound -French
Until all is over one's ambition never dies
Until death there is no knowing what may befall -Italian
Until he extends his circle of compassion to include all living things, man will not himself find peace -Albert Schweitzer
Until spring comes, nightingales do not sing -Azerbaijani
Until the lions have their historians, tales of the hunt shall always glorify the hunter -African
Until you have smoked out the bees, you can't eat the honey -Russian
Unwilling service earns no thanks -Danish
Unworthy offspring brag the most of their worthy descent -Danish
*Up in the morning early, avoids behavior surly*
*Up to sixteen, a lad is a Boy Scout. After that, he is a girl scout.*
Up, sluggard, and waste not life; in the grave will be sleeping enough -Ben Franklin
Upbraiding makes a benefit an injury -French
Upon a slight pretext the wolf takes the sheep -French
Upon an egg the hen lays an egg -French
Use a book as a bee does a flower
Use a short rope, a nice smile, and a hot brand -Will Rogers
Use cover or concealment as much as possible -US Marine
Use is a second nature
Use it or lose it -German
*Use it up, wear it out- make it do, or do without*
Use makes mastery
Use power to curb power -Chinese
Use soft words and hard arguments -English
Use the means, and God will give the blessing
Use your enemy's hand to catch a snake -Persian
Used properly, stumbling blocks can become stepping stones
Useful burdens become light

*Vagrants are at home everywhere*
Vain glory blossoms but never bears
Vainglory bears no grain -French
Value judgments are destructive to our proper business, which is curiousity and awareness -John Cage
Vanity blossoms but bears no fruit - Nepalese
Vanity has no greater foe than vanity -French
Vanity of vanities, all is vanity
Vanquishers are kings, the vanquished, thieves
Variety is the spice of life
Various are the roads to fame -Italian
*Velvet paws hide sharp claws*
Vengeance is mine, saith the Lord -Italian, Biblical
Venture a small fish to catch a great one - English
Venture all; see what fate brings -Vietnamese
Venture not to defend what your judgment doubts of -English
Verily, God will not change a people, until they first change themselves from within -Qur'an
Very good corn grows in little fields -French
Very hard times in the wood when the wolves eat each other -French
*Vessels large may venture more but little boats should keep near shore -* Ben Franklin
*Vessels large may venture more, But little boats must keep near shore* -French
Vetches seem bitter to the full-cropped pigeon -Italian
Vexations, duly borne, Are but as trials, which heaven's love to man sends for his good -Italian
Vice is learnt without a schoolmaster -Danish
Vice is most dangerous when it puts on the garb of virtue -Danish
Vices are their own punishment -Aesop
Vices may become virtues, as hatred is treasured in time of War
Victory belongs to the most persevering
Victory belongs to those who persevere
Victory goes to the player who makes the next-to-last mistake -Chessmaster Savielly Grigorievitch Tartakower
Vile let him be who deems himself vile -Portuguese
Vinegar catches few flies
*Violence and kindness, virtue and vice multiply by example's device* -Wampanoag
Violence begets violence
Violence treats even justice unjustly
Violence, like kindness, is a gift that keeps on giving- One experiences it, and then passes it on

Vipers breed vipers -Danish
Virtue alone is true nobility -William Gifford
Virtue and happiness are mother and daughter -Ben Franklin
Virtue flies from the heart of a mercenary man
Virtue in the middle, said the Devil, when seated between two lawyers
-Danish
Virtue is a jewel of great price -Portuguese
Virtue is a middle course between vices -Horatius
Virtue is fairer far than beauty
Virtue is found in the mean
Virtue is her/its own reward
Virtue is its own reward, and vice its own punishment
Virtue is like a rich stone, it's best plain set -Francis Bacon
*Virtue is not knowing, but doing* -Japanese
Virtue is not measured by special efforts, but by ordinary doing -Pascal
Virtue is the only true nobility
Virtue never grows old
Virtue which parleys is near a surrender
Vision and task joined are the hope of the world
Vision without action is a daydream. Action without vision is a nightmare
-Japanese
Vision without action is but a dream. Action without vision is drudgery.
*Vision, persistence, sense of urgency; all things are accomplished with*
*these three*
Visit rarely, and you will be more loved -Arabic
Visit your aunt, but not every day of the year -Spanish
*Visits always give pleasure - if not the arrival, the departure* -Portuguese
Visits should be short, like a winter's day
Vodka is the aunt of wine -Russian
Vows made in storms are forgotten in calms -English
Voyages shape youth -French
*Wade not in unknown water*
Wait, and sweet sunshine will be there -Japanese
Wait calmly. There's nothing to get excited or panic about. Your road in
life will open up to you of its own accord. –Akira Kurosawa
Wait not for dead men's shoes
Wait time and place to take your revenge, for it is never well done in a
hurry -Italian
Wait until it is night before saying that is has been a fine day -French
Wake not a sleeping cat -French
Wake not the sleeping lion
*Walk groundedly; talk profoundly; drink roundly; sleep soundly*
Walk lightly in the spring; Mother Earth is pregnant –Kiowa

Walk straight, my son - as the old crab said to the young crab -Irish
Walk till the blood appears on the cheek, but not the sweat on the brow -Spanish
*Walk ye now into thy fear- and it will sooner disappear*
*Walk your talk, or take a walk*
*Walls and Pitchers have ears*
Walls have ears, and little pots too -South African
Walls have mice and mice have ears -Persian
Walls have mice, mice, ears -Persian
Walls sink and dunghills rise -Portuguese
*Walnuts and pears you plant for your heirs* -Portuguese
Want a thing long enough and you don't -Chinese
Want and necessity break faith and oaths -Danish
Want is the mother of industry
Want of care does us more damage than want of knowledge
Want of rest is worse than want of wealth
*Want of variety leads to satiety* -Danish
Wanton kittens make sober cats -Danish
War begun, hell unchained -Italian
War does not determine who is right, war determine who is left
War ends nothing -Zairean
War is death's feast -George Herbert
War is good for business -Ferengi Rule of Acquisition
War is much too serious a matter to be entrusted to the military -French
War is sweet only to those who haven't experienced it -Latin
War is sweet to him who goes not to it -Portuguese
War is the business of barbarians
War makes robbers, and peace hangs them -Italian
Warm your socks over the fire if you want, but they still aren't biscuits -Will Rogers
Warning: dates on calendar are closer than they appear
*Wash a dog, comb a dog, Still a dog, remains a dog*
Wash your dirty linen at home
Wash your hands in the flowing Ganges -Hindi
Waste makes want -Hindi
Waste not, want not -Ben Franklin
Waste of time is the most extravagant and costly of all expenses
Watch the pennies and the dollars will take care of themselves
Watch your thoughts- They become words- Watch your words- They become actions- Watch your actions- They become habits- Watch your habits- They become character- Watch your character- It becomes your destiny
Watching what you say is your best friend -Arabic

Water afar [off] quenches not fire
Water after does not quench a fire at hand -Italian
Water and fire will not stop the determined man -Japanese
Water can float a boat, and sink it also -Chinese
Water does not run under a lying stone -Russian
*Water, dropping, day by day- wears the hardest rock away*
Water fills both square and circular pots -Japanese
Water flows not under settled stones -Russian
Water for oxen, wine for kings -Spanish
*Water run by will does not turn the mill*
Water under the bridge [returneth not]
Water washes everything -Portuguese
Water which is too pure has no fish -Ts'ai Ken T'an
Water, smoke, and a vicious woman, drive men out of the house -Italian
Waves will rise on silent water -Gaelic
We all do fade as a leaf
We all make mistakes
We are all Adam's children, but silk makes the difference -English
We are all angels, everyone's job is helping others
We are all equal before death -Maltese
We are all full of weakness and errors; let us mutually pardon each other
our follies -Voltaire [Francois-Marie Arouet]
We are all ignorant about different things -Will Rogers
We are all just crash dummies on the information highway -Steve Worona
We are all one child, spinning through Mother Sky –Shawnee
We are all related -Lakota
We are all visitors to this time, this place. We are just passing through.
Our purpose here is to observe, to learn, to grow, to love... and then we
return home -Aborigine
We are all well placed, said the cat, when she was seated on the bacon
-Danish
We are friends, we assist each other to bear our burdens -Osage
We are here and it is now. Further than that all human knowledge is
moonshine -H. L. Mencken
We are made from Mother Earth, and to her we return
–Shenandoah
We are made kind by being kind -Eric Hoffer
We are no more than candles burning in the wind -Japanese
We are not born for ourselves
We are only truly alive when we are connected -Kahlil Gibran
We are our habits. Excellence is not an act, but a habit -Aristotle
We are the beautiful colors of the flowers in the garden of the Creator,
who loves all the colors -Hopi

We are usually the best men when in the worst health -English
*We are what we daily do; excellence doth habit woo*
We arrive at the truth being skeptical -Abélard
We ask the heart what to do, and the head how to do it -Wampanoag
We boil at different degrees -Ralph Waldo Emerson
We can do no great things; only small things with great love -Mother Teresa
We can get better ideas in 2 hrs of 'creative loafing' than in 8 hrs at work
We can hold back neither the coming of the flowers nor the downward rush of the stream; sooner or later, everything comes to its fruition -Loy Ching-Yuen
We can live without a brother, but not without a friend
We can live without our friends, but not without our neighbors
We can only appreciate the miracle of a sunrise if we have waited in darkness
We can seldom get our children to do what we tell them, but they almost never fail to imitate us -Colin Powell
We cannot be more sensitive to pleasure without being more sensitive to pain -Alan Watts
We cannot escape fear. We can only transform it into a companion that accompanies us on all our exciting adventures -Susan Jeffers
We cannot really love anybody with whom we never laugh
- Agnes Repplier
We carry our neighbours' failings in sight; we throw our own crimes over our shoulders
*We control but our intention- from that, for us, doth flow creation*
We could save a lot if we could live as cheaply after payday as we did before
We do not care of what we have, but we cry when it is lost -Russian
We do not fear death, but the thought of death -Latin
We do not learn for school, but for life -Latin
We do not own the earth, we borrow it from our children -Native American
We do not remember days, we remember moments -Casare Pavese
We do not walk on our legs, but on our will -Sufi
We don't change the message, the message changes us
We don't kill a pig every day -Rumanian
We don't learn from school but from life -Latin
We fear things in proportion to our ignorance of them -Livy
We fear what we don't understand -Aesop
We first make our habits, and then our habits make us
We forfeit three fourths of ourselves in order to be like other people -Schopenhauer
We grow too soon old and too late smart -Amish

We have been taught to believe that negative equals realistic and positive equals unrealistic -Susan Jeffers

We have met the enemy, and he is us -Walt Kelly

*We have no more right to consume happiness without producing it, than to consume wealth without producing it*

We have not inherited this land from our ancestors; rather we have borrowed it from our children -Native American

We have not saddled and yet we are riding -Portuguese

We have nothing to fear but fear itself

We hope to grow old, yet we fear old age; that is, we are willing to live, and afraid to die

We know not what is good until we have lost it

We know so much more than I know by myself -Wampanoag

We know the worth of a thing when we have lost it -French

We learn by teaching -Seneca Philosophus, Italian

We learn little from victory, much from defeat -Japanese

We learn not at school, but in life

We learn not for school but for life -Seneca

We lie the loudest when we lie to ourselves

We make a living by what we get, but we make a life by what we give -Winston Churchill

*We may give without loving, but we cannot love without giving*

We may have all come on different ships, but we are in the same boat now -Martin Luther King

We may not change the direction of the wind, but we can adjust our sails

We most need patience when we least want it -Japanese

We must accept truth even if it changes our point of view -George Sand

We must all hang together, or assuredly we shall all hang separately -Ben Franklin

We must bear our cross with patience, said the man when he took his wife on his back -Danish

We must believe in luck. For how else can we explain the success of those we don't like? -Jean Cocteau

We must constantly build dikes of courage to hold back the flood of fear

We must eat a peck of dirt before we die -Danish

We must face what we fear; that is the case of the core of the restoration of health -Jawaharlal Nehru

We must have reasons for speech but we need none for silence -French

We must learn to walk before we can run -French

We must live by the living/quick, not by the dead

We must repeat a thousand and one times that perseverance is the only road to success

We must sow, even after a bad harvest -Danish

We must suffer much, or die young -Danish

We must take the bad with the good

*We must take things as they are, and not as we would wish from afar*
-Napoleon

We never know the worth/value of water till the well is dry -French

We never repent of having eaten too little –Thomas Jefferson

We only live once, but if we work it right once is enough

We ourselves create the truth -Latin

We seldom repent of having eaten too little

We shall be judged not by what we might have done, but by what we have been

We shall lie all alike in our graves

We shall never have friends if we expect to find them without fault

We shall see, as the blind man said -French

We shape clay into a pot, but it is the emptiness inside that holds whatever we want -Lao Tzu

We should be as water, which is lower than all things yet stronger even than the rocks -Oglala Sioux

We should be careful to get out of an experience only the wisdom that is in it - and stop there; lest we be like the cat that sits down on a hot stove-lid. She will never sit down on a hot stove-lid again---and that is well; but also she will never sit down on a cold one anymore -Mark Twain

We should be patient with everyone, but above all with ourselves

We should forgive our enemies, but only after they've been taken out and shot

We should learn as long as we may live [We live and learn] -Latin

We should never remember the benefit we have offered, nor forget the favour received

We should not pretend to understand the world only by the intellect; we apprehend it just as much by feeling. Therefore, the judgment of the intellect is, at best, only the half of truth, as must, if it be honest, also come an understanding of its inadequacy -Carl Jung

We should push our work, the work should not push us

We should weep for men at their birth and not at their death

We soon believe what we desire

We stand somewhere between the mountain and the ant -Onondaga

We still live in the garden, and when enough people realize this, the garden will bloom right where we are

We traded in shrouds; people stopped dying -Lebanese

We underestimate the power of touch, a smile, a kind word, a listening ear, an honest compliment, or the smallest act of caring, all of which have the potential to turn a life around -Leo Buscaglia

We were born to die anyhow -Mexican
We were called to be witnesses, not lawyers or judges
We will be grateful to flowers only if they have born fruits -Zimbabwean
We will be known forever by the tracks we leave –Dakota
Weak men had best be witty
Weak men wait for opportunity, but the strong men make it
Wealth and content are not always bedfellows -Ben Franklin
Wealth conquered Rome after Rome had conquered the world -Italian
Wealth is both an enemy and a friend -Nepalese
Wealth is but dung; useful only when spread -Chinese
Wealth is not his that has it, but his that enjoys it -Ben Franklin
Wealth is not his who makes it, but his who enjoys it -Italian
Wealth is not what we have, but what we are
*Wealth is nothing without health*
*Wealth makes health*
Wealth makes worship
Wealth may be an excellent thing, for it means power, leisure, and liberty
Wear the demeanor of a cat, and let not your heart be seen -Japanese
Weather forecasts are horoscopes with numbers
Weather, wind, women, and fortune change like the moon -French
*Wedlock is a padlock*
Wedlock rides in the saddle, and repentance on the crupper -French
Weeds need no sowing
Weeds never die out -Danish
Weeps the field because it does not get any seeds -Albanian
Weighty work must be done with few words -Danish
Welcome evil if thou comest alone
Welcome is the best cheer -Danish
Welcome thy neighbor into thy fallout shelter. He'll come in handy if you run out of food.
Welcome to the next level!
*Well begun is half done* - Aristotle
Well done is better than well said -Ben Franklin
Well fed but ill taught -French
Well fed, wed bred
*Well honed is half mown* -German
We'll never know the worth of water till the well go dry -Irish, Scottish
Well ordered charity begins with oneself -French
Well whetted/sharpened is half mowed
Well-conceived plans are a big step towards a job well done
Well-regulated charity begins with one's self -French
Well-timed silence hath more eloquence than speech -Martin Fraquhar Tupper

Went in at the one eare and out at the other  —John Heywood
Went in one ear and out the other -John Heywood, French
Were if not for "if" and "but," we should all be rich for ever -French
Were it a wolf it would spring at your throat -French
Were the devil to come from hell to fight, there would forthwith be a
Frenchman to accept the challenge -French
Wet behind the ears
What a man is at seven is also what he is at seventy -Turkish
What a monk thinks he dares to do -French
What a neighbor gets is not lost -French
What a sauce for the goose is sauce for the gander
What a woman wills, God wills -Spanish
What an old man sees, seated, a small child cannot see even standing on
top of a mountain -Nigerian
What ardently we wish, we soon believe -Edward Young
What belongs to everybody belongs to nobody -Spanish
What breaks in a moment may take years to mend -Swedish
What can you say about a society that says that God is dead and Elvis is
alive? -Irv Kupcinet
*What cannot be cured must be endured* - Edmund Spenser
What children hear at home, soon flies abroad
What children say, they have heard at home -Wolof
What comes from the fife goes back to the drum -French
What costs little is little esteemed -Italian
What do we live for if not to make life a little less difficult for others?
What do you expect from a pig but a grunt?
What does not kill me makes me stronger —Goethe
What does not poison, fattens -Italian
What does the moon care if the dogs bark at her?
What doesn't kill you, makes you stronger -Nietszche
What eats you is within your dress -Swahili
What eyes don't see, the heart doesn't feel -Portuguese
What fills the eye fills the heart -Irish
What flares up fast, extinguishes soon -Turkish
What goes around, comes around
What goes up must come down
What good is a pretty dish, if it is empty
What good is honor when you are starving -Yiddish
What good is running when you're on the wrong road?
-German
What good shall I do this day? What good have I done today?
What has a beginning has an end. What begins in the world of form must
also end in it.  1 of 7 Universal Principles -George Ohsawa

What has a front has a back. What has a top has a bottom, what has a left side has a right side. 2 of 7 Universal Principles -George Ohsawa

What has not been, may be -Italian

*What heart can think, or tongue express, The harm that groweth of idleness?* –John Heywood

What hurts, often instructs

What I have done is due to patient thought

What I have in my heart is brought out by the wine -Albanian

What I learned I don't remember. What little I know I have guessed -N. Chamford

What is a rebel? A man who says no -Albert Camus

What is a workman without his tools?

*What is an epigram? A dwarfish whole, its body brevity, and wit its soul –* Coleridge

What is another's always sighs for its master -Portuguese

What is bad for one is good for another -French

What is bred in the bone will not out of the flesh   -Portuguese

What is brought by the wind will be carried away by the wind -Persian

What is done by night appears by day

*What is done cannot be undone*

*What is done well enough, is done quickly enough*

What is enough was never little -French

What is good for the goose is good for the gander

What is got by begging is dearly bought -Danish

What is gotten over the devil's back is spent under his belly -Danish

What is in the marrow is hard to take out of the bone -Irish

*What is known to three is known to everybody*

What is learned in the cradle lasts till the grave -French

What is learnt in the cradle is carried to the grave

What is natural cannot be bad -Latin

What is new is always fine -French

*What is new is not true, what is true is not new*

What is not wisdom is danger

What is on a sober man's mind is on a drunk's tongue -Russian

What is one man's cloud is another man's sunshine

What is past and cannot be prevented should not be grieved for –Pawnee

What is play to the cat is death to the mouse -Danish

What is play to the strong is death to the weak -Danish

What is sauce for the goose is sauce for the gander

What is serving God? Tis doing Good to Man - Ben Franklin

What is sweet in the mouth is not always good in the stomach -Danish

What is the probability that something will happen according to the odds?

*What is there sadder under the sun- than a day that is gone and nothing*

done
*What is true by lamplight is not always true in sunlight* - French
What is true for you is what you have observed yourself
What is true is not always probable -French
What is wealth good for, if it brings melancholy?
What is worth doing at all is worth doing well
*What is worth receiving is worth returning* -French
What is written without effort is read without pleasure -Samuel Johnson
What Jupiter may do, the ox[people] may not -Roman
What keeps out the cold keeps out the heat -Italian
*What lies behind us and what lies before us are tiny matters compared to what lies within us*
What lives nearest the heart is first in the mouth
What makes life dreary is the want of motive
What may be done at any time will be done at no time -Scottish
What may not be altered is made lighter by patience
-Horace
What men wish, they like to believe -Latin
What most people want, young or old, is not merely security, or comfort, or luxury, although they are glad enough to have these. Most of all they want MEANING in their lives. If our era and our culture and our leaders do not, or cannot, offer great meanings, great objectives, great convictions, then people will settle for shallow and trivial substitutes -Rockefeller Report on Education
*What must be must be*
What one dishes out, he must also eat -German
What one hopes for is always better than what one has -Ethiopian
What one knows it is sometimes useful to forget -Latin
What other people do or say is their stuff; how we react is our stuff
What sculpture is to a block of marble, education is to the soul
What seven can do with a spoon, one can do with a plough -Russian
What signifies knowing the names, if you know not the natures of things -Ben Franklin
*What soberness conceals, drunkenness reveals*
*What sobriety conceals, alcohol reveals*
What the child does, the child is -Irish
What the child hears at the fireside is soon known at the parish church -French
What the child sees, the child does –Irish
*What the child, when young, receives- passes on, and gladdens, or it grieves*
What the colt learns in youth he continues in old age -French
What the eye does not see, the heart does not grieve over -French

*What the eye sees not, the heart craves not*
What the farmer doesn't know, he doesn't eat -Dutch
*What the fool does at last, the wise man does at first* -Portuguese
What the fool does at the end, the wise man did at the beginning
What the gauntlet wins, the gorget consumes -French
What the heart is full of, the mouth runs over with -Dutch
What the heart knows today the head will understand tomorrow -James Stephens
What the heart knows today, the head will know tomorrow
What the heart thinks, the tongue speaks -Romanian
What the kings wills, that the law wills
What the people believe is true -Anishinabe
What the she-wolf does/brings forth pleases the he-wolf -Spanish
What the sober man keeps in his heart, is on the tongue of the drunkard -French
What the sober man thinks, the drunkard tells -Dutch
What the soldier said isn't evidence -Dutch
What the young one begs for, the grown-up throws away -Russian
What this country needs is more people to inspire others with confidence, and fewer people to discourage any initiative in the right direction; more to get into the thick of things, fewer to sit on the sidelines merely finding fault; more to point out what's right with the world,and fewer to keep harping on what's wrong with it;and more who are interested in lighting candles, and fewer who blow them out -James Keller, founder, the Christophers
*What to children is remitted- to the country is transmitted*
What was hard to bear is sweet to remember -Portuguese
What was hard to endure is sweet to recall -French
What was is no more, what is just is -Maltese
What water gives, water takes away -Portuguese
*What we acquire without sweat, we give away without regret*
What we are ignorant of is immense
What we do in life reverberates throughout eternity -Maximus the Gladiator
What we do not understand we do not possess
What we do willingly is easy
What we first learn, we best know
What we learn with pleasure we never forget
What we lose in hake we shall have in herring
What we see depends mainly on what we look for
What we've been longest used to is most likely to agree with us best
What will be, will be -Italian
What you can't get is just what suits you -French

What you can't have, abuse -Italian
What you cannot avoid, welcome - Chinese
What you concentrate on soon will grow
What you dislike in another, take care to correct in yourself
What you do to others will bear fruit in you -Singhalese
What you do today may be the only sermon some people hear today -St. Francis
What you do yourself is well done -Danish
What you don't know won't hurt you -German
What you don't see with your eyes, don't invent with your mouth -Jewish
What you give away you keep -Kurdish
What you give is what you get
What you give you get, ten times over -Yoruba
What you have, hold -John Heywood
What you learn to your cost you remember long -Danish
What you lose on the swings you gain/get back on the roundabouts
What you make of your life is up to you –Rule 8 of 10 Life Rules
What you put out comes back
What you resist you become -Taoist
What you see in yourself is what you see in the world -Afghan
What you see is what you get
What you see is what you intend to do about it -David Rioch
*What you see outside that's true- exists already within you*
What you seem to be, be really - Ben Franklin
What you spend, you have -Afghan
*What you think about, you bring about*
What you would seem to be, be really -Ben Franklin
What youth is used to, age remembers
What youth learns, age does not forget -Danish
*What you've got, you've got -German*
What! give the lettuce in charge to the geese!
*What's done is done*
*What's lost is lost*
What's the point? -Ladakh [proverb to drain anger]
Whatever God's dream about humanity may be, it seems certain it cannot come true unless humanity cooperates -Stella Terrill Mann
Whatever happens, all happens as it should
Whatever I do, I will do in my power
Whatever is begun in anger ends in shame -Benjamin Franklin
Whatever is in the heart will come up to the tongue -Persian
Whatever is not nailed down is mine. What I can pry loose is not nailed down -Collis P. Huntington
Whatever is worth doing at all is worth doing well

-Philip Dormer Stanhope
Whatever is written on the forehead is always seen -Arab
Whatever it is, I fear the girls, even when they kiss -Latin
Whatever man had done, man may do -Palestinian
Whatever the boss says goes
Whatever you do, do cautiously, and look to the end -Latin
Whatever you do, do with all your might
*Whatever you do, do with your might; Things done by halves are never done right*
Whatever you do, have a good time doing it!
Whatever you learn, you learn it for yourself -Latin
Whatever you sow, you reap -Persian
Whatever your painful memory- That was Then. This is Now.
Whatever you're ready for is ready for you -Mark Victor Hansen
What's bred in the bone will come out in the flesh -English
What's done by night appears by day
*What's done cannot be undone*
*What's done is done* - French
What's everybody's work is nobody's work -Portuguese
What's good for the goose is good for the gander -Irish
*What's good is often forgotten; what's bad is often hidden* -Norwegian
What's in it for me?
What's learnt in the cradle lasts till the tomb
*What's lost is lost*
*What's mine is mine,* and what's yours is mine too -Ferengi Rule of Acquisition
What's more miserable than discontent?
What's right is what's left if you do everything wrong
-Robin Williams
What's to me today, tomorrow to you -Latin
What's up your sleeves?
What's yours is mine, and what's mine is my own
Whatsoever ye would that men should do to you, do ye ever so to them
-Biblical
When a blind man carries a lame man, both go forward -Swedish
When a camel is at the foot of a mountain, then judge of his height -Hindi
When a cat wants to eat her kittens, she says they look like mice -Kurdish
When a cow is lost it is something to recover its tail, were it only to make a handle for one's door -French
When a dog is drowning, everyone offers him drink
When a dog runs away, hit him! hit him!
When a father helps a son, both smile; but when a son must help his father, both cry -Jewish

When a favor is shown to a white man, he feels it in his head, and his tongue speaks out; when a kindness is shown to an Indian, he feels it in his heart, and the heart has no tongue -Shoshone

When a female has tears in her eyes, the one who cannot see is the male

When a finger points at the moon, the imbecile looks at the finger -Chinese

When a flight is proceeding incredibly well, something was forgotten -Pilot wisdom

When a fox walks lame, the old rabbit jumps –Oklahoma

When a friend asks, there is no tomorrow

When a knave is in a plum-tree, he has neither friend nor kin

When a leader loses power, his followers become disorganized -Chinese

When a man begins to reason, he ceases to feel -French

When a man has fallen into the mire, the more he flounders, the more he fouls himself -Italian

When a man is coming toward you, you need not say, "Come here -Twi [Ghana]

When a man is in a sack, he must get out at the mouth or at the bottom -Danish

When a man is not liked, whatever he doth is amiss -Danish

When a man is wealthy he may wear an old cloth -Twi [Ghana]

When a man is willing and eager, the gods join in –Aeschylus

When a man moves away from nature, his heart becomes hard –Lakota

When a man prays one day and steals six, the Great Spirit thunders, and the evil one laughs –Oklahoma

When a man wants to murder a tiger, it's called sport; when the tiger wants to murder him, it's called ferocity -George Bernard Shaw

When a man's heart is full of fire, sparks fly out of his mouth

When a man's coat is threadbare, it is easy to pick a hole in it -Twi [Ghana]

When a man's friend marries, all is over between them -French

When a man's wife learns to understand him, she usually stops listening to him

When a miser dies, the heirs feel as happy as when they kill a pig -Maltese

When a mouse makes fun of a cat, there is a hole -Senegalese

*When a musician hath forgotten his note, He makes as though a crumb stuck in his throat* -Senegalese

When a person takes one step toward God, God takes more steps toward that person than there are sands in the worlds of time -The Work of the Chariot

When a proud man hears another praised, he feels himself injured

-English
*When a task is once begun, never leave it till it's done*
When a thief kisses you, count your teeth -Yiddish
When a thing is done, advice comes too late -Romanian
When a tree is falling, every one cries, down with it -Italian
When a twig grows hard it is difficult to twist it. Every beginning is weak -Irish
When a twig grows hard it is difficult to twist it –Irish
*When Adam delved and Eve span, who was then the gentleman?*
When ale/drink/wine is in, wit is out
*When all is said and done, usually more is said than done*
When all men say you are an ass, it is time to bray -Slavic
When all men speak, no man hears
When all other sins are old, avarice is still young -French
When all sins grow old, covetousness is young -French
When all you have is a hammer, everything looks like a nail -French
When an elder speaks, be silent and listen –Mohawk
When an elephant is in trouble even a frog will kick him - Hindi
When an opportunity is neglected, it never comes back to you
When anger blinds the eyes/mind, truth disappears -Danish
When anger rises, think of the consequences -Confucius
When angry, count ten, before you speak; if very angry, an hundred – Thomas Jefferson
When appetite commands, the pocket pays
*When asked a question you don't want to answer, ask "Why do you want to know?", smile and banter*
*When bad be your prospects, don't still still and cry, instead jump up and say to yourself, I'll try*
When bulls fight, woe to the frogs -Portuguese
When cat and mouse agree, the farmer has no chance -Danish
When choosing between two evils I like to try the one I've never tried before -Mae West
When dirt comes to honour, it knows not what to be -Danish
When drink is in, wit is out
When eating a fruit, think of the person who planted the tree -Vietnamese
When eating bamboo sprouts, remember the man who planted them -Chinese
When elephants fight, the grass is trampled -African
When every man gets his own, the devil gets nothing -Danish
*When every one minds his own [business] the work is done* -Danish
When everybody says you are drunk, go to sleep -Italian
*When everybody's somebody, then nobody's anybody*
*When everything is a priority, nothing is a priority*

When faced with a bad choice, pick the lesser of two evils
When fire is applied to a stone, it cracks -Irish
When flatterers meet, the devil goes to dinner
When fools go to market the huckster gets money -Danish
When fortune calls, offer her a chair - Yiddish
When fortune comes, open your doors -Italian
When fortune knocks upon the door open it widely -Spanish
When fortune knocks, open the door
When fortune smiles, embrace her
When fortune smiles, she often designs the most mischief
When fortune turns against you, even jelly breaks your teeth - Iranian
When fortune's chariot rolls easily, envy and shame cling to the wheels
-Danish
When friends ask, there is no tomorrow -Danish
When glory comes, memory departs -French
When God gives bread, the people give butter -Polish
When God sends flour the devil carries off the sack -French
When god will punish, he will first take away the understanding
When going from hot air to cold air, breathe through the nose
When gold speaks, every tongue is silent -Italian
*When good cheer is lacking, friends will go packing*
*When good cheer is lacking, our friends will be packing*
-Italian
When goods increase, the body decreases -French
When Greek meets Greek, then comes the tug of war -French
When guns speak, it is too late to argue
When his head is broken he puts on his helmet -Italian
*When house and land are gone and spent, then learning is most
excellent* -Italian
When I am working on a problem I never think about beauty. I only think
about how to solve the problem. But when I have finished, if the solution
is not beautiful, I know it is wrong -Buckminster Fuller
When I dare to be powerful – to use my strength in the service of my
vision – then it becomes less and less important whether I am afraid
-Audre Lorde
When I despair, I remember that all through history the way of truth and
love has always won. There have been tyrants and murderers and for a
time they seem invincible, but in the end, they always fall -- think of it,
ALWAYS -Mohandas K. Gandhi
When I eat your bread, I sing your song -German
When I follow my dreams, confidently and without hesitation, the right and
perfect people, opportunities and experiences show up
When I have money in my purse, I have food in my mouth -Danish

When I hear I see, when I see I hear -Zen koan
*When I lent, I had a friend; but when I asked, he was unkind*
When I was younger I could remember anything, whether it had happened or not -Mark Twain
When ideas fail, words come in very handy -Goethe
When ill luck falls asleep let nobody wake her -Italian
When I'm dead, everybody's dead, and the pig too -Italian
When in doubt, do now
*When in doubt, leave out*
When in doubt, abstain -French
When in doubt, communicate!
When in doubt, do nothing -George John Whyte-Melville
When in doubt, do the friendliest thing
When in doubt, gallop! -French Foreign Legion
When in doubt, lie -Ferengi Rule of Acquisition
When in doubt, play trumps
When in doubt, seek the silence
When in doubt, wait
When in doubt, whip it out
When in Rome, do as the Romans do
When Indians ran this country, men could hunt and fish any time they liked, women did all the work, and there were no taxes.  White man thought he could improve on a system like that -Cherokee
When it comes time to die, be not like those whose hearts are filled with the fear of death, so when their time comes they weep and pray for a little more time to live their lives over again in a different way. Sing your death song, and die like a hero going home -Chief Aupumut, Mohican
When it pours upon the parson, it drops upon the clerk -Danish
When it rains porridge, the beggar has no spoon -Danish
When it thunders, the thief becomes honest -Italian
When its time has arrived, the prey becomes the hunter -Persian
When joy is in the parlour, sorrow is in the passage -Danish
When knaves fall out, honest men get their goods. When Priests dispute, we come at the Truth -Ben Franklin
When lazy horses begin to start, old women to dance, and white clouds to rain, there is no stopping them -Danish
When life's path is steep, keep your mind even - Horace
When love and skill go together, expect a masterpiece
-John Ruskin
When love is not madness, it is not love -Spanish
When love puts in, friendship is gone
When machines go wrong they remind you of how powerful they are
When mistrust enters, love departs -Danish

When money talks, the truth is silent -Russian
*When need is highest, God's help is nighest*
When neighbours quarrel, lookers-on are more apt to add fuel than water -Danish
When no appropriate Rule applies, make one up! -Ferengi Rule of Acquisition
When one beats the dog, a lion is also afraid -Polish
When one dog barks another will join it -Latin
When one door shuts, another opens
When one foot stumbles, the other is near falling -Danish
When one has not what one likes, one must like what one has -French
When one is about to act, one must reason first
When one is dead, it is for a long while -French
When one is hungry, everything tastes good
When one is in love, a cliff becomes a meadow -Ethiopian
When one is prepared, difficulties do not come -Ethiopian
When one shears the sheep, the skin on the ram trembles -Polish
When one shears the wethers, the goats are pleased -Polish
When one shuts one eye, one does not hear everything -Swiss
When others blow your horn, the sound carries twice as far -Will Rogers
When people ask me, "What do you do?" I say I create crisis, because crisis is that edge where change is possible -Lisa Fithian
When poverty comes in at the door, love flies out of the window
When pumpkins are watered, brinjals[small plants] also get watered -Kashmiri
When riches increase, the body decreases
When rogues/thieves fall out, honest men come by their own -Kashmiri
When rogues go in procession, the devil carries the cross -Italian
When someone asks you a question you don't want to answer, smile and ask, "Why do you want to know?"
When sorrow is asleep, wake it not
When sorrows come, they come not single spies, but in battalions
When spider webs unite, they can tie up a lion -Ethiopian
When spring is dancing among the hills, one should not stay in a little dark corner
When stomach is hungry, eyes are blind -Arabic
When strangers start acting like neighbors, communities are reinvigorated -Ralph Nader
When strict with oneself, one rarely fails -Confucius
When strong drink/alcohol enters, wisdom departs
When stupid man is doing something he is ashamed of, he always declares that it is his duty

When the angels present themselves, the devils abscond -Egyptian
When the ant says "ocean," he speaks of a puddle -Afghan
When the apple is ripe it will fall - Irish
When the beer goes in, the wits go out -Danish
When the belly is full, the mind is amongst the maids -Danish
When the belly is full, the bones would be at rest
When the blind man carries the banner, woe to those who follow -French
When the cage is ready, the bird is flown -French
When the candles are out, all women are fair -Polish
When the cat and mouse agree, the grocer is ruined -Persian
When the cat is absent, the mice dance
*When the cat is away, the mice will play*
When the cat's away, the mice dance -Italian
When the cat's stomach is full, the rat's back is bitter -Haitian
When the character of a man is not clear to you, look at his friends
-Haitian, Japanese
When the child is christened you will have godfathers enough -French
When the cock is drunk, he forgets about the hawk -Twi
When the cook is roasting for the butler, woe to the master's wine-cask
-Danish
When the cord is tightest, it is nearest snapping -Danish
When the crane attempts to dance with the house she gets broken bones
-Danish
When the devil finds the door shut, he goes away -Spanish
When the devil grows old, he turns hermit -French, Italian
When the devil says his paternosters, he means to cheat you -French
When the dog is drowning every one brings him water -French
When the door closes, something else opens
When the door is low one must stoop -French
When the drop/drink is inside, the sense is outside -Irish
When the elephants fight it is the grass that suffers
-Nigerian
When the fish is caught, the net is laid aside
When the fox cannot reach the grapes he says they are not ripe -Greek
When the fox licks his paw, let the farmer look after his geese -Danish
When the fox preaches, then beware your geese
When the fox preaches to the goose, her neck is in danger -Danish
When the fox preaches, look to/take care of the geese -German
When the fox preaches, take care of yourselves, hens -Italian
When the fox sleeps, no grapes fall in his mouth
When the Frenchman sleeps, the devil rocks him -French
When the friar's beaten, then comes James -French
*When the fruit is scarcest, its taste is sweetest*

*When the furze is in bloom, my love's in tune* -French
When the game is most thriving it is time to leave off -Danish
When the going gets tough, the tough change the Rules -Ferengi Rule of Acquisition
When the going gets tough, the tough get going
When the goose trusts the fox, then woe to her neck -Danish
When the gorse is out of bloom, kissing's out of fashion -Danish
When the government fears the people, we have liberty. When the people fear the government, we have tyranny
When the hand ceases to scatter, the heart ceases to pray -Irish
*When the hand is clean, It needs no screen* -Irish
When the head aches, all the body is the worse
When the head aches, all the limbs ache -Danish
When the head aches, all the members partake of the pain -Cervantes
When the heart is afire, some sparks will fly out at the mouth
When the heart is at ease, the body is healthy -Chinese
When the heart is full, the tongue will speak -Scottish
When the helm is gone the ship will soon be wrecked -Danish
When the host smiles most blandly he has an eye to the guest's purse -Danish
When the house is burned down, you bring water
When the iron is hot, strike -John Heywood
When the legends die, the dreams end, there is no more greatness – Shawnee
When the lion is dead the hares jump upon his carcass -Italian
When the lion's skin falls short, piece it out with that of the fox -Italian
When the liquor was gone, the fun was gone -Irish
When the manger is empty, the horses fight -Danish
When the millers are making an uproar, do you tie up your sacks -Italian
When the moon is full, it begins to wane -Japanese
When the mouse has had enough, the meal is bitter -Danish
When the mouse laughs at the cat, there is a hole nearby -Nigerian
When the music changes, so does the dance -Hausa
*When the music's playin' is when it's time to be dancin'* -Country wisdom
When the next house is on fire, 'tis high time to look to your own -Nigerian
*When the night's darkest, the dawn's nearest*
When the only tool you own is a hammer, every problem begins to look like a nail
*When the outlook is poor, try the uplook*
When the pear is ripe, it falls -Italian, Slavic
When the pig has had a bellyful, it upsets the trough -Dutch
When the pig is proffered, hold up the poke -Rumanian
When the pin is pulled, Mr. Grenade is not our friend - U.S. Marine Corps

When the pirate prays, there is great danger -Dutch
When the pot boils over, it cooleth itself -Dutch
When the pupil is ready to learn, a teacher will appear -Zen
When the pupil is ready, the teacher will come -Chinese
When the rooks are silent, the swans begin to sing -Danish
When the sale is made, shut up
When the sea turned into honey, the poor man lost his spoon -Bulgarian
When the shepherd strays, the sheep stray -Dutch
When the ship has sunk, everyone knows how she might have been saved -Italian
When the sky falls, we'll all catch larks -Irish
When the smoke alarm goes off, dinner is served
When the soul wishes to experience something she throws an image of the experience out before her and enters into her own image -Meister Eckhart
When the stomach is full, the heart is glad -Dutch
When the student is ready, the master appears -Oriental
When the sun comes in, the doctor goes out
When the sun shines on thee, thou needest not care for the moon -Italian
When the sun shineth, make hay -John Heywood
When the sword of rebellion is drawn, the sheath should be thrown away -English
When the tiger kills, the jackal profits -Afghan
When the tree falls, every one runs to cut boughs -Dutch
When the tree falls, any child can climb it -Vietnamese
When the tree falls, the monkeys scatter -Chinese
When the tree is down, every one runs to it with a hatchet to cut wood -Italian
When the tree is down, everybody runs to the branches -French
When the tree is fallen, every one runs to it with his ax
When the wagon is tilting, everybody gives it a shove -Danish
When the well is full, it will run over
When the well's dry, we know the worth of water -Ben Franklin
When the will is prompt, the legs are nimble -Italian
*When the wind is in the east, 'tis neither good for man nor beast* -Italian
When the wind serves, all aid -Italian
*When the winds of death do blow, then are equal, high and low*
When the wine goes in, the wit goes out -Dutch
*When the wine is in the man, the wit is in the can* -Dutch
When the wine is in, the wit is out -Rumanian, Italian
When the wisdomkeepers speak, all do well to listen –Seneca
When the wolf grows old, the crows ride him -Dutch
When the wolf's ears appear, his body is not far off -Danish

When the word is in the mouth, you must caress the sheath -Danish
When the words are said, the holy water is made -French
When the wound is healed, the pain is forgotten -Danish
When there is a fire in the neighborhood, carry water to your own house -Italian
When there is little bread at table, put plenty on your plate -Italian
When there is no enemy within, the enemies outside cannot hurt you -African
When there is no wind, every man is a pilot -French
When there is nothing, the church loses -Italian
When there is order in the nation, there will be peace in the world -Chinese
When there is room in the heart, there is room in the house -Danish
When there's no Law, there's no Bread - Ben Franklin
When they are silent, they cry out -Cicero
When thieves fall out, the peasant recovers his goods -Danish
When thieves fall out, the thefts are discovered -French
When thieves fall out, honest men come to their goods -Dutch
When thieves fall out, their knaveries come to light -Portuguese
When thine enemy retreateth, make him a golden bridge -Dutch
When things are at the worst, they begin to mend -Dutch
When things go well, it is easy to advise -Dutch
When three know it, all know it
When thy neighbour's house is on fire, it's time to look about thee -Dutch
*When two agree in their desire, One sparke will set them both on fire* -English
When two do the same thing, it isn't the same [one can get away with doing something while another cannot] -Terentius
When two dogs fight for a bone, the third runs away with it -Dutch
When two enemies blow one horn, the third will have to suffer for it -Danish
When two fall out/fight, the third wins
When two friends have a common purse, one sings and the other weeps
When two quarrel, both are in the wrong -Dutch
When two quarrel, both are to blame -Dutch
When two ride on one horse, one must sit behind
When Want comes in at the door, Love flies out at the window -Dutch
When war begins, then hell opens
When we are back from backing up the backups, the system will be back up
When we are flat on our backs, there is no way to look but up
When we cannot get what we love, we must love what is within our reach -French

*When we know our inner purpose- all of life is then in focus*
When we have gold we are in fear; when we have none we are in danger
When we least expect it, the hare darts out of the ditch -Dutch
When we respect other living things, they respond with respect for us – Arapaho
When we sing everybody hears us, when we sigh nobody hears us -Russian
When we think we lead, we are most led -Henry James Byron
When we understand deeply in our hearts, we will fear and love and know the Great Spirit -Oglala Sioux
When what you want doesn't happen, learn to want what does -Arabic
When wine enters, modesty departs -Italian
When wine goes in, the truth comes out -Spanish
When wine is in, truth/wit is out
When wine sinks, words swim -Italian
When wisdom fails, luck helps -Danish
When wise men play mad pranks, they do it with a vengeance -Italian
*When woman reigns, the devil governs* -Italian
When written in Chinese, the word 'crisis' is composed of two characters-- one represents danger and one represents opportunity
*When you are an anvil, hold you still; when you are a hammer, strike your fill* -Polish
When you are dead, your sister's tears will dry as time goes on, your widow's tears will cease in another's arms, but your mother will mourn you until she dies -Arabic
When you are deluded and full of doubt, even a thousand books of scripture are not enough. When you have realized understanding, even one word is too much.
When you are ready to learn, a teacher will appear
When you are right, you can afford to keep your temper
When you are well off, keep as you are -French
When you begin to dislike someone, do something nice for him
When you believe you are excusing yourself, you are accusing yourself -St. Jerome
When you can do the common things in life in an uncommon way, you will command the attention of the world -George Washington Carver
*When you commit with all your heart- The Universe will do its part*
When you die, you will be spoken of as those in the sky, like the stars -Yurok
When you do not have any work, move the door -Albanian
When you drink water, remember the mountain spring -Chinese
When you fall into a pit, you either die or get out -Chinese

When you feel all steamed up, remember the teakettle- it is always up to its neck in water, and yet it sings

When you find a sacred cow, milk it for all it is worth

*When you find your beloved inside you, you will find your beloved beside you* -Alan Cohen

When you follow your bliss...doors will open where you would not have thought there would be doors; and where there wouldn't be a door for anyone else -Joseph Campbell

When you get into a tight place and everything goes against you, till it seems as though you could not hold on a minute longer, never give up then, for that is just the place and time that the tide will turn

When you get there, there isn't any there there -Sheng-ts'an

When you get to the end of your rope, tie a knot and hang on

When you get to the top of the mountain, keep climbing -Chinese

When you get to your wit's end, you'll find God lives there

When you go to a donkey's house, don't talk about ears -Jamaican

When you go to buy, use your eyes, not your ears -Czech

When you go to dance, take heed whom you take by the hand -Danish

When you go within, you will never be without

When you have a lot of balls in the air, it's essential to remember which ones are glass

When you have a lot to do, start with a meal -South African

When you have a talent of any kind, use it, care for it, guard it –Sauk

When you have eliminated the impossible, that which remains, however improbable, must be the truth -Sir Arthur Conan Doyle

When you have given nothing, ask for nothing -Albanian

When you have learned about love, you have learned about the Creator – Fox

When you have no choice, mobilize the spirit of courage -Jewish

When you have only two pennies left in the world, buy a loaf of bread with one, and a lily with the other -Chinese

When you hear hoofbeats, think horses, not zebras

When you help someone up a hill, you're that much nearer the top yourself

When you hit the wall of blankness and despair, like Bodhidharma, stare at the wall, patiently, until a path opens up -Akira Kurosawa

When you journey within, you will never be without

When you know a man, you know his face, but not his heart –Seneca

When you live next to the cemetery you cannot weep for everyone -Russian

When you lose the rhythm of the drumbeat of the Creator, you are lost from the peace and rhythm of life –Cheyenne

When you lose, don't lose the lesson

When you love others, you aren't nervous -Mary Martin
When you meet a man, you judge him by his clothes; when you leave, you judge him by his heart -Russian
When you reach the end of your rope, tie a knot and hang on
When you realize you've made a mistake, take immediate steps to correct it
When you say one thing, the clever person understands three - Chinese
When you say, "I love you," mean it
When you say, "I'm sorry," look the person in the eye
When you see a palm tree, the palm tree has seen you -African
When you see a rattlesnake poised to strike, strike first –Navajo
When you see a snake, never mind where he came from
When you see a turtle on top of a fence post, you know he had some help -African
When you see clouds gathering, prepare to catch rainwater -Gola [African]
When you see the handwriting on the wall, you can bet you're in a public building
When you see the wolf, do not look for his track -Italian
When you speak badly about others, you are telling who you are yourself
When you taste honey, remember gall -Ben Franklin
When you think of yourself as a hammer, everything else looks like a 20-penny nail
When you throw dirt, you lose ground -Texan
When you wallow with pigs, expect to get dirty -Country wisdom
When you want to test the depth of a stream, don't use both feet -Chinese
When you were born you cried and the world rejoiced. Live your life so that when you die, the world cries, and you rejoice -Cherokee
When you're all wrapped up in yourself, you're a small package
*When you're with your fiancee' with tradesmen, know her voice and way- when her finger sports the wedding ring, the same tune, to you, will she sing*
When your devil was born, mine was going to school -Italian
When your enemy falls, don't rejoice- but don't pick him up either -Yiddish
When your mouth is closed, you can't put your foot in it
When your work speaks for itself, don't interrupt
When you're average, you're as close to the bottom as to the top
When you're getting kicked from behind, that means you're in front
When you're good to others, you are best to yourself
When you're sad, learn something -Merlin
When you're thirsty, it's too late to think about digging a well - Japanese
When you've boxed yourself in, there is no sunshine
Whenever I am brokenhearted. I emerge more compassionate -Sylvia

Boorstein
Whenever I have to decide between two evils, I always choose the one I haven't tried before –Mae West
Whenever people agree with me, I always feel I must be wrong -Oscar Wilde
Whenever you exploit someone, it never hurts to thank them. That way, it's easier to exploit them the next time -Ferengi Rule of Acquisition
Whenever you feel abandoned, you are abandoning yourself the most at the moment
Whenever you find yourself on the side of the majority, it is time to pause and reflect - Mark Twain
Where a man feels pain, he lays his hand -Dutch
Where a man never goes, there his head will never be washed -Danish
Where drums beat[there is war], laws are silent
Where every hand fleeceth, the sheep goes naked
Where every man is master, the world goes to wreck -Polish
Where fear is present, wisdom cannot be -Lactantius
Where God has his church, the Devil will have his chapel -Spanish
Where goeth the needle, so followeth the thread -Russian
Where gold speaks, every tongue is silent -Slavic
Where I make my living, there is my home -Somalian
Where is the knowledge we have lost in information? -T.S. Eliot
Where is the unity, there is the victory -Latin
Where is there a tree not shaken by the wind? - Armenian
Where law lacks, honor should eke it out -Danish
Where little is known, little is required
Where love fails, we espy all faults
Where love is, there is faith
Where love is, there the eye is -Italian
Where might is master, justice is servant
Where misfortune befalls, injuries follow -French
Where money and counsel are wanting, it is best not to make war -Danish
Where no counsel is, the people fall; but in the multitude of counselors there is safety -Biblical
Where nothing is, the king must lose his right
Where nothing is, nothing can be had
*Where nought's to be got, kings lose their scot*
Where old age is evil, youth can learn no good -English
Where one door shuts, another opens
Where passion is high, there reason is low
Where poverty comes in at the door, loves flies out at the window -Dutch
Where remedies are needed, sighing avails not -Italian
Where shall a man have a worse friend than he brings from home -Italian

Where shall the ox go but he must labour, since he knows how?
Where shall the ox go, and not have to plough?
Where something is thin, that's where it tears -Russian
Where the bird was hatched, it haunts -Dutch
Where the carcass is, there shall the eagles be gathered together -Polish
Where the carrion is, there the eagles gather -Danish
Where the cock is, the hen does not crow -Portuguese
Where the dam leaps over, the kid follows
Where the devil cannot put his head, he puts his tail -Italian
Where the dike/dam is lowest the water first runs over -Dutch
Where the fir tree is hauled, people grab branches, where there is success, everyone has a part in it -Finnish
Where the goat is tied, she must browse -French
Where the heart loves, there the legs walk -Maltese
Where the hedge is low, every one will cross it -Italian
Where the hedge is lowest, every one goes over -Dutch
Where the hedge is lowest, men jump over -French
Where the hedge is lowest, men may soonest over
Where the hostess is handsome, the wine is good -French
Where the knot is loose, the string slips
*Where the plow shall fail to go, there the weeds will surely grow*
Where the Pope is, there is Rome -Italian
Where the pupil is willing; the teachers will appear -Italian
Where the ship goes, the brig can go -Italian
Where the skin of the lion does not suffice, we must join that of the fox -Italian
Where the sun entered/enters, the doctor does not
Where the thread is weakest, it breaks -French
Where the tongue slips, it speaks the truth -Irish
*Where the wasp has passed, the fly sticks fast* -French
Where the wound is, the plaster must be
Where there are bees, there is honey -Albanian
Where there are no dogs, the fox is a king -Italian
Where there are no swamps, there are no frogs -German
Where there are no tigers, a wildcat is very self-important -Korean
Where there are reeds, there is water
Where there are too many cooks, the soup will be too salty -Italian
Where there are women and geese, there wants no noise -Polish
Where there is a sea, there are pirates -Greek
Where there is a will, there is a way
Where there is an open mind, there will always be a frontier
Where there is discipline, there is virtue; where there is peace there is plenty -Danish

Where there is equality, there never can be perfect love -Italian
Where there is great doubt, there will be great awakening; small doubt, small awakening, no doubt, no awakening -Zen saying
Where there is great love, there is great pain -Italian
Where there is harmony, there is victory -Latin
Where there is heart, there are hands -Albanian
Where there is least heart, there is most tongue -Italian
Where there is life, there is hope -Portuguese
Where there is little bread, cut first -Portuguese
Where there is love, there is pain -Spanish
Where there is love, even a hut seems like heaven -Russian
Where there is marriage without love, there will be love without marriage -Ben Franklin
*Where there is no burning Vision- is no useful sort of action*
Where there is no fire, no smoke rises -Portuguese
Where there is no good within, no good comes out
Where there is no honor, there is no dishonor -Portuguese
Where there is no honor, there is no grief -Slavic
*Where there is no sore, there needs no plaster* -French
Where there is no vision, the people perish -Bible, Proverbs 29:18
Where there is no wit within, no wit will come out -Danish
Where there is nothing, the king loses his rights -French
Where there is smoke, there is fire
Where there is sugar, there are bound to be ants -Malay
Where there is true hospitality, few words are needed -Arapaho
Where there's a will, there's a way
Where there's a will, I want to be in it
Where there's life, there's hope - Theocritus
Where there's music, there can be love -French
Where there's no fire, there's no smoke -Portuguese
Where there's no good within, no good comes out -Dutch
*Where there's no might, there's no right -Portuguese*
*Where there's reek, there's heat*
Where there's smoke, there's fire -Latin
Where they saw chance, we see law
Where we least think, there goeth the hare away -Slavic
Where will is right, law is banished -Danish
Where you cannot climb over, you must creep under -Danish
Where you feel good, there is your home -Latin
Where you tell your secret, you surrender your freedom -Portuguese
Where you were a page, be not an esquire -Portuguese
Where you were born is less important than how you live - Turkish
Where your will is ready, your feet are light -Romanian

Wheresoever the carcass is, there will the ravens be gathered together
Wherever he is satisfied with what he does, he has reached his culminating point-he will progress no more
Wherever I connect with God, that is my home
Wherever there is a human being there is an opportunity for kindness -Seneca
Wherever you go, go with all your heart -Confucius
Wherever you go, there you are -Buckaroo Banzai
Wherever you go, you can't get rid of yourself -Polish
Whether the pitcher strikes the stone, or the stone the pitcher, it is bad for the pitcher -Portuguese
Whether you think that you can, or that you can't, you are usually right -Henry Ford
While there is life, there is hope
While I breathe, I hope -Cicero
While men teach, they learn
*While the cat's away, the mice will play* -James Ray
While the dogs yelp, the hare flies to the wood -Danish
While the grass grows, the horse starves
While the grass is growing, the mare dies -Danish
While the great bells are ringing, no one hears the little ones -Danish
While the priest climbs a post, the devil climbs ten
While the word is in your mouth, it is your own; when 'tis once spoken, 'tis another's
While the word is yet unspoken, you are master of it; when once it is spoken, it is master of you -Arabic
While there's life, there's hope -Italian
While two dogs are fighting for a bone, a third runs away with it -Italian
While we breathe, there is hope
While you are proclaiming peace with your lips, be careful to have it even more fully in your heart -Francis of Assisi
Whilst the dogs are growling at each other, the wolf devours the sheep -French
Whilst the tall maid is stooping, the little one sweeps the house -Portuguese
*Whilst we drink, prank ourselves, with wenches daily, Old age upon us at unawares doth sally* -Portuguese
Whisper your way to success -Ferengi Rule of Acquisition
Whispering tongues poison truth
*Whistling girls and crowing hens come soon to a nasty end*
White man bring bad spirits to Indian.  After Indian die, bad spirits go back to white man.  -Native elder
White man chase money and things like dog chase squirrel, but he never

have enough.  White man so much money, starving for more money.
White man live in head, always worry, always afraid, always take.  White
man forget his heart.  White man no alive.  White man crazy. -Native
elder
White man chief eat so good, but white man children no much food.
Indian chief not eat till Indian children full of food.  Who the real chief?
-Native elder
White man elects clowns for leaders, and then wonders why his
government is a circus.  White man crazy -Aninishnabe
White man forget nature, think only about money, and drink to forget his
emptiness inside.  Indian not think about money, love nature, and know
rapture in nature.  White man say Indian stupid.  Who [is] the stupid one?
White man forget to love children.  White man hurt his children so much,
the hurt pass on, then hurt them more in prison.  White man hurt hurt hurt
people, then wonder why the people hurt hurt hurt other people.  Why
white man so blind? -Native elder
White man give alcohol to Indian, Indian get sick, die, white man take
Indian land, say Indian no goo drunk.  White man drink alcohol too.  Who
is taking land from the white man? -Native elder
White man gives his children liquor, cars, and no love, and his leaders
power, money, and no respect.  White man crazy -Aninishabe
White man gives his money to the bank, his children to the school, his
labor to his job, his house to the mortgage,  his friends up for money, his
happiness for things, and then wonders why he is empty inside.  White
man crazy -Chief Two Trees
*White man hate his job, hate his wife, hate his children, hate his life*
White man lost and sad, feel bad for before, fear for coming.  White
woman no talk happy with other white woman much, no sing when she
work.  White woman sad, make white man sad.  Make children sad.
White man crazy. -Native elder
White man loves things, and beats his children.  White man let his head
tell him what to do, and his heart how to do it.  White man crazy
-Aninishnabe
White man no sense -Aninishnabe
White man not know all women beautiful.  White man make the white
woman ugly.  White man crazy. -Native American
White man work so hard, for two week vacation live like Indian live all the
time. -Native elder
White man punish the poor people who steal a little, and reward the rich
people who steal a lot.  White man crazy -Aninishnabe
White man so many books, so small wisdom, so empty heart -Scagticoke
White man steal so much because afraid, white man no help the white
man.  Indian poor, but Indian help Indian.  White man have so much,

white man sad, afraid. Indian have so little, indian happy, big heart, because Indian help Indian. White man so much book, so small wisdom. Indian so small book, so much wisdom. Who the smart? -Native elder
White man take so many medicines, like food. Indian take food, as medicine. White man pay so much money for the medicine, but always sick. The Indian, no money for doctor, always healthy.
White man trust newspaper and television, not his own heart. White man want the soft lie, not hard truth. White man crazy -Dakota
White meal is not got out of a coal-sack -French
White men have too many chiefs –Nez Perce
Whither goest thou, Misfortune? To where there is more -Portuguese
Who accepts, sells himself -Italian
Who answers for another pays -French
Who answers suddenly knows little
Who are a little wise, the best fools be -John Donne
*Who are ready to believe- are easy to deceive*
Who asks a question is a fool for a minute; who asks not remains a fool for an eternity -Chinese
Who asks isn't wrong  -Latin
Who ate the Sultan's raisins will pay it back as a date -Arabic
Who begins too much accomplishes little -German
Who benefits? To whose profit is it? Cui bono? -Latin
*Who betrays me once wrongs me day or night, who betrays me twice doth serve me right*
Who blows his nose too hard makes it bleed -French
Who builds on the mob builds on sand -Italian
*Who buys, has need of eyes* -Italian
Who buys land buys war -Italian
Who buys wants a hundred eyes, who sells need have but one -Dutch
*Who can escape envy and blame, that speaks or writes for public fame?*
Who cannot beat the ass, beats the saddle -Spanish
Who cannot beat the horse, let him beat the saddle -Italian
Who cannot work out his salvation by heart will not do it by book -French
Who changes country changes luck -Italian
Who changes his condition changes fortune -Italian
Who chastises his child will be honoured by him, who chastises him not will be shamed -Dutch
*Who chatters to you will chatter of you* -Slavic
Who comes last to the pot is soonest wroth
*Who comes seldom, is welcome* -Italian
Who could live without hope?
Who dangles after the great is the last at table and the first to be cuffed -Italian

Who depends on another man's table often dines late -Italian

Who digs a trap will fall into it -Arabic, Biblical

*Who divides honey with the bear, will be like to get the lesser share* -Italian

Who does all he may, never does well -Italian

*Who does good shall receive good* -Portuguese

Who does not beat his own child will later beat his own breast -Persian

Who does not thank for little will not thank for much -Estonian

Who does not venture gets neither horse nor mule, and who ventures too much lose horse and mule -French

Who does not wish to be like the wolf, let him not wear its skin -Italian

Who does not work, is heavy to the earth -Albanian

Who does too much, often does little -Italian

Who does well, encounters well -Dutch

Who doesn't keep faith with God won't keep it with man -Dutch

Who doubts, errs not -French

Who draws [a cart] is urged on

Who draws his sword against his prince must throw away his scabbard -French

Who eats capon, capon comes to him -French

Who eats his fowl alone, must saddle his horse alone -Portuguese

*Who enjoys skiing downhill had best enjoy climbing uphill* -Russian

Who errs in the tens errs in the thousands -Italian

*Who excuses himself accuses himself* -Italian

Who excuses himself without being accused makes his fault manifest -Italian

*Who excuses, accuses* -Dutch

Who faints not, achieves -Portuguese

Who fears no shame comes to no honour -Dutch

Who fears wolves goes not to the woods -Russian

Who frequents the kitchen smells of smoke -Italian

Who gives sell, sells dear, if the receiver be not a churl -Italian

Who gives to me, teaches me to give -Dutch

Who gives, teaches a return -Italian

Who glows not, burns not -Italian

Who goes a beast to Rome, a beast returns -English

*Who goes aborrowin' shall soon go asorrowin, and who gives out loan shall soon know groan* -Benjamin Franklin

Who goes and returns makes a journey -French

Who goes fasting to bed will sleep but lightly -Dutch

Who goes himself is in earnest, who sends is indifferent -Italian

*Who goes not, sees not; who proves not, believes not* -Italian

Who goes softly goes safely, and he that goes safely goes far -Italian
*Who goes to doctor, heavy of purse- will the sooner, leave by hearse*
Who hangs himself in the chimney should not complain of smoke
Who has a bad wife, his hell begins on earth -Dutch
Who has a choice, has a problem -German
Who has a tongue in his head can go all the world over -Italian
Who has a trade, has a share everywhere
Who has but one eye must take good care of it -Dutch
Who has deceived thee as oft as thyself? -Ben Franklin
Who has gold is a welcome guest
Who has love in his heart has spurs in his sides -Italian
*Who has made the error, need not blame the other* -Hindi
Who has many servants has many thieves -Dutch
Who has neither fools nor beggars nor whores among his kindred, was born of a stroke of thunder -Ben Franklin
*Who has never done thinking never begins doing* -Italian
Who has never tasted bitter, knows not what is sweet
Who has no authority, has no opinion -Arabic
Who has no children does not know what love is -Italian
Who has no haste in his business, mountains to him seem valleys
Who has no head should have legs -Italian
Who has no heart, has no heels -Albanian
Who has no money in his purse must have honey in his mouth -Italian
Who has no money must have no wishes -Italian
Who has no plagues makes himself some -Italian
Who has no shame all the world is his own -Italian
Who has no thirst has no business at the foundation -Dutch
Who has not, is not -Italian
Who has not understanding, let him have legs
Who has not, cannot -French
Who has nothing, is nothing -Italian
Who has nothing need fear to lose nothing
Who has patience, has all things
Who has patience may get fat thrushes at a farthing apiece -Italian
Who has patience sees his revenge -Italian
Who has plenty of pepper may pepper his beans -Dutch
Who has skirts of straw needs fear the fire
Who has something, is something -Italian
Who has, is -Italian
Who hath built with sweat, shall defend with blood -Albanian
Who hath little shame, the world is all his own -Italian
Who hath no courage must have legs -Italian
Who hath no horse may ride on a staff

Who hears but one bell hears but one sound -French
Who hears music feels his solitude -French
Who holds his peace and gathers stones, will find a time to throw them -Portuguese
Who holds the fault doth stand on guard
*Who holds the purse rules the house*
Who hurries much, falls much -Arabic
Who is born a fool is never cured -Italian
Who is born of a cat will run after mice -French
Who is in fear of every leaf must not go into the wood -Italian
Who is in the right fears, who is in the wrong hopes -Italian
Who is lazy today, regrets it tomorrow -Albanian
Who is mighty? He who makes an enemy into a friend -Hebrew
*Who is mocked, soon matures, but for mockers, are no cures* -Finnish
Who is present at a wrongdoing and lifts not a hand to prevent it is as guilty as the wrongdoers -Omaha
Who is rich? He that enjoys his portion -Ben Franklin
Who is righteous overmuch is a morsel for the Old One -Dutch
Who is satisfied with his fortune?
Who is shy dies from hunger -Albanian
Who is silent seems to agree -Latin
Who is strong? He that can conquer his bad habits -Ben Franklin
Who judges others, condemns himself -Italian
Who keeps company with a wolf will learn to howl -Italian, Rumanian
Who knows how to praise knows also how to lie -Albanian
Who knows most speaks/says least -Spanish
Who knows most, forgives most -Italian
Who knows most, knows least -Italian
Who knows not how to dissemble, knows not how to live
Who knows not how to dissemble, knows not how to reign -Italian
Who knows not how to flatter knows not how to talk -Italian
Who knows not how to pray, let him go sail the sea -Italian
Who knows not the game, let him not play -Italian
Who knows nothing doubts nothing -French
Who knows the tongues is at home everywhere -Dutch
Who knows what is to be tired, does not know how to be -'not tired' -Albanian
Who knows you not, values you not –Swahili
Who laughs at others' ills, has his own behind the door -Italian
Who leaves the old way for the new, will find himself deceived
Who lends to a friend loses doubly -French
Who lets the rams graze gets the wool -Albanian
Who lies down with dogs gets up with fleas -Italian, Latin

Who lives by hope will die by hunger
Who lives content with little possesses much
*Who lives on the score has shame evermore* -French
Who lives will see -French
Who looks at beauty, and sees it not, shall look at wealth, and see it not -Yoruba
Who looks not before finds himself behind -French
Who loses liberty loses all
Who loves me, loves my dog too -Latin
Who loves the tree loves the branch -Italian
*Who loves to roam may lose his home* -Italian
Who loves well chastises well -Italian
Who loves well is slow to forget -French
Who loves, believes -Italian
Who loves, fears -Italian
Who makes everything right must rise early
Who makes the dough will also cook -Albanian
Who makes the wolf his companion should carry a dog under his cloak -Italian
Who minds his own business has no time to mind other folks
Who more busy than they who have least to do?
*Who more than he is worth doth spend, he makes a rope his life to end*
Who moves, picks up, who stands still, dries up -Italian
*Who never tries cannot win the prize*
Who offends writes on sand; who is offended, on marble -Italian
Who often changes, damages -French       ·
Who opens a school door closes a prison -French
Who paints me before blackens me behind -Italian
Who pardons the bad, injures the good
Who pays a debt creates capital -Italian
*Who pays beforehand is served behindhand* -Italian
Who pays soon borrows when he will -French
Who pays the piper calls the tune -French
Who places the sign, "no silver hidden here", does not keep thieves away -Chinese
*Who pours his purse into his head- of thieves worries, not in bed* -Benjamin Franklin
Who promises much and does little, dines a fool on hope
Who proves too much proves nothing -French
Who punishes one threatens a hundred -French
Who receives a gift sells his liberty
Who reckons without his host must reckon again -Dutch
*Who refuses, muses* -French

Who remove stones bruise their fingers
Who repairs not his gutter, repairs his whole house
Who rises late must trot all day -French
Who rubs the chicken, eats even the egg -Albanian
Who runs is followed -Dutch
Who runs with wolves soon learns to howl
Who saves, saves for the cat -Italian
Who says A must say B -Italian
Who says nothing is impossible? Some people do it every day!
Who seeds winds will reap storms -Portuguese
Who seeks more than he needs hinders himself from enjoying what he has -Hebrew
Who sees the face sees not the heart -Portuguese
*Who serves everybody gets thanks from nobody*
Who serves his fellows is of all the greatest –Dakota
*Who serves the mass is thanked by none, but cursed if aught is left undone* -French
Who serves the public serves a fickle master -Dutch
Who serves the public, serves no one -Italian
Who serves well and says nothing makes claim enough -Italian
Who serves well asks enough -French
Who shall guard the guards themselves? Iuvenalis
Who shall live, shall see -French
Who sleeps warmly, feels even cold -Albanian
Who sows ill, reaps ill -Italian
Who sows, reaps -French
Who sows thorns, let him not walk barefoot -French, -Italian
Who speaks, sows; who listens, reaps -French
Who spits against heaven, it falls on his head -French
Who spits against the heaven, it falls in his face
Who spits against the wind spits in his own face -French
Who spits against the wind, fouls his beard -Dutch
Who stays under the tree, eats the fruits -Albanian
Who steals an old man's supper does him no wrong
*Who swells in prosperity will shrink in adversity*
Who swims in sin shall sink in sorrow
Who swings an aggressive sword will be killed by it -Arabic
Who takes a lion at a distance fears a mole present -Italian
Who takes an eel by the tail and a woman at her word, may say he holds nothing -Italian
Who takes his teachings and applies them increases his knowledge
Who tastes syrup for the first time soon is sticky -Portuguese
Who tends the fence tends also the farm

Who throws a stone at the sky, it falls back on his head -Italian
*Who to-day was a haughty knight, is to-morrow a pennyless wight* -Dutch
Who travels for love finds a thousand miles not longer than one -Dutch
Who travels will also get tired -Albanian
Who troubles others has no rest himself -Italian
Who undertakes many things at once seldom does anything well -Dutch
Who undertakes too much, succeeds but little -Dutch
*Who ventures to lend, loses money and friend* -Dutch
Who waiteth for dead man's shoes will go long barefoot
-John Heywood
Who wants all, loses all
Who wants fire, let him look for it in the ashes -Dutch
Who wants to beat a dog, soon finds a stick -Dutch
Who watches not, catches not -Dutch
Who watches the watchmen? Juvenal
*Who weds a sot to get his cot, will lose the cot and keep the sot* -Dutch
*Who will in time present pleasure refrain, shall in time to come the more
pleasure obtain* -Portuguese
*Who will not keep a penny, shall never have many*
Who will not when he can, can't when he will -Portuguese
Who wishes for a short Lent let him contract debts to be paid at Easter
-Italian
Who wishes to travel far spares his steed -French
*Who wives for a dower, resigns his own power* -French
Who won't be ruled by the rudder must be ruled by the rock -French
Who would be young when he is old, must be old when he is young
Who would eat fish, must get wet -Russian
Who would have a clear head must have a clean stomach
Who would have many friends, let him test but few -Italian
Who would not have feet set on his neck, let him not stoop -Italian
*Who would regard all things complacently- must wink at a great many*
-Dutch
Who writes, reads twice -Latin
Who, what, where, with what, why, how, when? Quis, quid, ubi, quibus
auxiliis, cur, quomodo, quando?
Whoever brings finds the door open for him -Italian
Whoever desires is always poor -Latin
Whoever gossips to you will gossip about you -Spanish
Whoever has a tail of straw should not get too close to the fire -Latin
American
Whoever has the best data doesn't necessarily win. Whoever manipulates
the data best wins -Statistical maxim
Whoever has the gold makes the rules

Whoever said the pen is mightier than the sword never encountered automatic weapons -General MacArthur

Whoever saves one [human] saves the whole world -Talmud

Whoever teaches his son teaches not only his son but also his son's son, and so on to the end of generations -Hebrew

Whoever wins the war gets to write the history

Whom a serpent has bitten, a lizard alarms -Slavic

Whom fortune wishes to destroy, she first makes mad

Whom God will help, none can hinder

Whom God will help, nothing does harm

Whom God would ruin, he first deprives of reason

Whom the gods love die young

Whom the gods would destroy, they first make mad -Greek

Whom we love best, to them we can say least -English

Whose bread I eat, his song I sing -German

Whose stick, his buffalo - Hindi

Whoso hath land hath war -French

Whoso hunteth with cats will catch nothing but rats -Dutch

Whoso is tired of happy days, let him take a wife -Dutch

Whoso is well let him keep so -French

Whoso learneth young forgets not when he is old

Whosoever draws his sword against the prince must throw the scabbard away -French

Why are you laughing? Change the name and the story is about you -Horatius

Why be difficult, when with a bit of effort, you can be impossible?

Why beholdest thou the mote that is in thy brother's eye, but considerest not the beam that is in thine own eye?

Why buy a cow if you can get the milk for free -French

Why buy a cow when milk is so cheap?

Why does the white man create a demon inside himself, to drive him to sickness and craziness, called Time? -Hopi Indian

Why gild the lily?

Why keep/have a dog and bark yourself?

Why kill time when one can employ it?

Why not go out on a limb? Isn't that where all the fruit is?

Why not seize the pleasure at once? How often is happiness destroyed by preparation, foolish preparation! -Jane Austen

Why not upset the apple cart? If you don't, the apples will rot anyway

Why pay for the cow when the milk is free?

Why seek a doctrine? As soon as you have a doctrine, you fall into dualistic thought -Huang Po

Why should it matter that one bowl is dark, and another, pale, if each is of

good design, and serves its purpose well? -Hopi
Why should the devil have all the best tunes?
Wicked men obey from fear; good men, from love
Wickedness does not go altogether unrequited
Wide ears and a short tongue [are the best]
*Widows give much happiness; divorced women, but distress*
Wilful waste makes woeful want
Will he nill he, the ass must go the fair -Portuguese
Will is character in action
Will is power -French
Will laugh well who will laugh the last -French
Willing is not enough, we must do -Johann Von Goethe
Willows are weak, yet serve to bind bigger wood -Italian
Win a bet of your friend, and drink it on the spot -Portuguese
Win or lose, there's always luxuries -Ferengi Rule of Acquisition
Win some, lose some
Wind and fortune are not lasting -Portuguese
Wine and judgment mature with age
Wine divulges truth -Irish
Wine in the bottle does not quench thirst
Wine is a turncoat, first a friend, then an enemy -Rumanian
Wine is mirror of the mind
Wine poured out is not wine swallowed -French
Wine wears no breeches -Spanish
Wine wears no mask -Spanish
Wine will not keep in a foul vessel -French
Wink at small faults- remember thou hast great ones -Ben Franklin
Winners accept responsibility for their lives
Winners are flexible, and try new things
Winners are losers who got up and gave it one more try -Dennis
DeYoung
Winners are patient
Winners are positive thinkers who see good in all things. From ordinary,
they make extraordinary.
Winners are positive thinkers who see good in all things. Winners are
people like you who persisted.
Winners believe in the path they have chosen
Winners blame neither fate for their failures nor luck for their success
Winners expect to win in advance.  Life is a self-fulfilling prophecy.
Winners fall but don't stay down
Winners know their strengths and weaknesses, and use them accordingly
Winners never quit, quitters never win –Vince Lombardi
Winners persist

Winners seek solutions, losers look for someone to blame

Winners take chances

Winter comes fast on the lazy -Irish

Wipe the nose of your neighbour's son, and marry him to your daughter -Portuguese

Wipe your sore eye with your elbow -Portuguese

Wisdom comes only when you stop looking for it, and start living the life the Creator intended for you –Hopi

Wisdom comes with age

Wisdom doesn't necessarily come with age. Sometimes age just shows up all by itself -Tom Wilson

*Wisdom in the man, patience in the wife, brings peace to the house, and a happy life -Dutch*

*Wisdom in the mind is better than money in the hand*

Wisdom is a good purchase, though we pay dear for it -Dutch

*Wisdom is better than gold or silver*

Wisdom is better than strength

Wisdom is easy to carry, but difficult to gather -Czech

Wisdom is more to be envied than riches

Wisdom is ofttimes nearer when we stoop than when we soar -William Wordsworth

Wisdom is only found in truth

Wisdom is the least burdensome traveling pack -Danish

Wisdom is to live in the present, plan for the future and profit from the past

Wisdom is to the mind what health is to the body

Wisdom is what's left, when everything learned is forgotten

Wisdom rides upon the ruins of folly -Danish

*Wisdom soon awareness seizes- great minds seek out great ideas*

Wise care begets care

Wise lads and old fools were never good for anything -Italian

Wise men change their minds, fools never -Italian

Wise men don't need advice. Fools won't take it.

Wise men have their mouth in their heart, fools their heart in their mouth

Wise men know more than they tell. Fools tell more than they know.

Wise men learn by other men's harms; fools, by their own.

Wise men learn by other men's mistakes/harms; fools by their own -Ben Franklin

Wise men love truth, whereas fools shun it

Wise men make proverbs, but fools repeat them without thinking -Samuel Palmer

Wise men sue for offices, and blockheads get them -Dutch

Wise men talk because they have something to say; fools talk because

they have to say something -Ben Franklin
Wise rats run from a falling house -Dutch
Wise sayings often fall on barren ground; but a kind word is never thrown away -Arthur Helps
Wish not so much to live long as to live well -Ben Franklin
Wishes are the echo of a lazy will -Dutch
Wishes never filled the bag -French
*Wishes won't wash dishes*
Wishing brings no autumn glory, nor does it cause winter to cease – Kiowa
*Wit bought is better than wit taught*
Wit is cultured insolence - Aristotle
Wit is folly, unless a wise man hath the keeping of it -Arabic
Wit is the lightning of the mind
Wit is the only wall between us and the dark -Mark Van Doren
*Wit once bought is worth twice taught*
Wit without learning is like a tree without fruit
Witches and harlots come out at night. -English
With a good name, one may easily sin -Dutch
With a stout heart, a mouse can lift an elephant -Tibetan
With all things and in all things, we are relatives –Dakota
With an old husband's hide one buys a young one -French
With art and knavery we live through half the year; with knavery and art we live through the other -Italian
With care, you realize your opportunity -Arabic
With enough 'ifs' we could put Paris in a bottle -French
With foxes, we must play the fox
*With honour and store, what would you more* -Dutch
With ifs, one would put Paris in a bottle –French
With law must the land be built -Danish
With lies you may go ahead in the world-but you can never go back -Russian
With money you are a dragon; with no money, a worm -Chinese
With money you can build a road in the sea -Maltese
With the absence of real men, there is no use for the swords -Arabic
With the fox, one must play the fox -Italian
With the good, we become good -Dutch
With the Gospel, men may become heretics -Italian
With the help of an If you might put Paris into a bottle -French
*With the old Almanack and the old Year, Leave thy old Vices, tho ever so dear* - Ben Franklin
With the skin of the dog, its bite is cured -Italian
With time, patience and art, the leaf of the mulberry-tree becomes satin

With time and straw medlars ripen -Italian
With time even a bear can learn to dance -Yiddish
With voting, boycotting in protest clearly makes the problem worse rather than better -Jane Auer
*With wishing comes grieving* -Italian
Without a friend, the world is a wilderness
Without a shepherd, sheep are not a flock -Russian
*Without bread and wine, even love will pine* -French
Without business, debauchery -French
Without Ceres and Bacchus, Venus grows cold -Slavic
Without confidence, there is no friendship
Without danger, we cannot get beyond danger
Without debt, without care -Italian
Without health, life is not life, life is lifeless
Without hope, the heart would break
Without justice, courage is weak -North American
Without kindness, there can be no true joy -Thomas Carlyle
Without method, little can be done to any good purpose
Without order, nothing can grow or expand
Without respect, love cannot go far
Without sleep, no health
Without Software, Hardware is useless
Without wind, grass does not move
Without Wisdom, wealth is worthless
Witticisms spare no one -French
Wives need to see the best in their men, or their marriages are vulnerable to other women who will
Wives serve, brothers inherit -Ferengi Rule of Acquisition
Woe be to an evil eye -Danish
Woe be to him whose advocate becomes his accuser -Danish
Woe to him that is alone
Woe to the vanquished! -Latin
Woe to thee, o land, when thy king is a child!
Woeful is the household that wants a woman
*Woes unite foes*
Wolves are often hidden under sheep's clothing -Danish
Wolves do not eat each other -Italian, French
Wolves don't eat wolves -Italian
Wolves have howled at the moon for centuries, yet it is still there -Italian
Woman [decides], impromptu; man, on reflection -Italian
Woman happy, everyone happy -Native American
Woman is a mystery to man, but are wise to each other
Woman, wind, and luck soon change -Portuguese

*Woman's intuition comes from paying attention*
Women always speak the truth, but not the whole truth -Italian
Women and cats will do as they please, and men and dogs should relax and get used to the idea -Robert A. Heinlein
Women and elephants never forget
Women and glass are always in danger -Portuguese
Women and hens are lost by too much gadding -Italian
*Women and their wills are dangerous ills*
*Women and wine, while they laugh, they make men pine*
Women are as changeable as the wind -Polish
Women are strong when they arm themselves with their weaknesses
Women are supernumerary when present, and missed when absent -Portuguese
Women are wise impromptu, fools on reflection -Italian
Women do not drink liquor, but it disappears when they are present -Irish
*Women easily upset, who vex  are denied their regular sex- a woman who is always smiling  knows enthusiastic loving* –Hispanic
Women have a lot of courage, or many of them would never get married
Women in mischief are wiser than men
Women in state affairs are like monkeys in glass-houses -Irish
*Women in their twenties will only look at dandies, when thirty will look at who is dirty, at forty five will take any man alive*
Women know a point more than the devil -Italian
Women like silent men. They think they're listening -Marcel Archard
Women naturally deceive, weep and spin -Italian
Women rouge that they may not blush -Italian
Women seldom repeat gossip- the way they heard it
*Women talk with other women- or they do frustrate their men* -Native American
Women who seek to be equal to men lack ambition
Women, asses, and nuts, require strong hands -Italian
*Women, money, and wine have their balm and their harm* -French
Women, priests, and poultry, never have enough -Italian
*Women's complaints, ax blows to a tree- the toppling must come, eventually*
Women's tears are a fountain of craft -Italian
Wonder is the beginning of wisdom -Greek
Wonders are many, and nothing is more wonderful than man
Wonders will never cease -Greek
Woods have ears and fields have eyes -Dutch
Word by word, the big books are made -French
Words and feathers the wind carries away
*Words are but sands; 'tis money buys lands* -French

Words are but wind
Words are female, deeds are male -Italian
Words are for women, actions for men -Italian
Words are like eggs: when they are hatched they have wings -Madagasy
Words are like spears: Once they leave your lips they can never come back -Yoruban
Words are mere bubbles of water; deeds are drops of gold -Tibetan
Words are the leaves of the tree of language, of which, if some fall away, a new succession takes their place -French
Words are the voice of the heart –Tuscarora
Words are windows to the heart
Words bind men
Words cut/hurt more than swords
Words fly away, the written letter remains -Latin
Words fly, writings remain
Words have no wings, but they can fly a thousand miles -Korean
Words have wings, and cannot be recalled
Words instruct, illustrations lead -Latin
Words move people, examples draw/compel them -Latin
Words must be weighed, not counted -Polish
Words of wisdom come from the mouths of simple people -Arabic
Words once spoken can never be recalled -Wentworth Dillon
Words once spoken cannot be wiped out with a sponge -Danish
Words pay no debts
Words should be weighed, not counted -Yiddish
*Words spoken are like eggs broken* -Sheri Glewen
Words that soak into your ears are whispered, not yelled -Country wisdom
Words won't feed cats -Italian
Work and you will be strong; sit and you will stink - Moroccan
Work as if you don't need money, love as if you've never been hurt, dance, as if nobody can see you, sing, as if no one can hear, live, as if the Earth was a heaven
Work as if you were to live a hundred years, Pray as if you were to die tomorrow - Ben Franklin
Work bears witness who does well
Work before pleasure -German
Work done expects money -Portuguese
Work expands so as to fill the time available
Work hard, keep the ceremonies, live peaceably, and unify your hearts – Hopi
*Work has a bitter root, but sweet fruit*
Work is a fire for frozen fingers

Work is love made visible -Kahlil Gibran
Work is only well done when it is done with a will
Work is the finest escape from boredom ever devised
Work is the medicine for poverty -Yoruban
Work is the most eloquent of any speech[actions are louder than words]
-Arabic
Work makes the workman
Work today, for you know not how much you may be hindered tomorrow
Work together to accomplish more -Latin
Work will not kill a man but worry will
Workaholics Unanimous Myth #5: There is only one best way
Working brings blessing -German
Working without a plan is sailing without a compass
*Worldly good is ebb and flood* -Dutch
Worldly prosperity is like writing on water -Telugu
Worry does not empty tomorrow of its sorrow; it empties today of its
strength -Corrie ten Boom
Worry is interest paid on trouble before it falls due
Worry is like a rocking chair- it gives you something to do, but it doesn't
get you anywhere -Dorothy Galyean
Worry is like gunning your engine in idle; lots of stress, but you don't get
anywhere -Country Wisdom
Worry kills more men than work
*Worry not for the future,  The present is all that thou hast, The future*
*soon will be present,  And the present will soon be the past*
*Worry not of children's ears- they watch you, let that stoke your fears*
Worry often gives a small thing a big shadow -Swedish
Worrying is like paying interest on a debt you may not owe
Worrying never changed anything
Worse than hardness of heart is softness of head
Worthless people blame their karma -Burmese
*Would you be of goal reminded  ignore all who are small minded  Follow*
*great ones up ahead, look to where you would be led*
*Would you learn, go out and play; struggle is the harder way*
Would you have me serve you, good king, give me the means of living
-Portuguese
Would you have potatoes grow by the pot-side?
Would you help others? Learn compassion. Would you help yourself?
Learn compassion -Dalai Lama
Would you know your daughter? See her in company -Portuguese
*Would you, long in life, endure- alternate your rest and labour*
Wouldn't it be funny if all the good and evil we did in life was like money in
the bank, given back to us, in one lump sum, as we entered the next

world?

Wrap yourself together in a carpet and roll together with your kinsmen -Azerbaijani

Write down the advice of him who love you, though you like it not at present -English

Write injuries in dust, benefits in marble - Ben Franklin

Write injuries in dust, but kindnesses in marble -French

Write it on your heart every day is the best day of the year

Write the wrongs done to you in sand, and the good things in marble -Arabic

Wrong laws make short governance

Wrong-doing quickly brings the curse and halts the blessing -Arabic

*Yard by yard, it's very hard, but inch by inch, and it's a cinch*

Yeah, though I walk through the valley of death I will fear no evil, [for I am the meanest son of a bitch in the valley]

*Year of snow, fruit will grow* -English

Years and sins are always more than owned -Italian

Years bring wisdom

Years know more than books -Italian, Slavic

Years wrinkle the skin, but lack of enthusiasm wrinkles the soul -Norman Vincent Peale

Yee have many strings to your bowe –John Heywood

Yesterday is a canceled check, tomorrow is a promissory note; today is money in the bank

Yesterday is but a dream, tomorrow is but a vision. But today well lived makes every yesterday a dream of happiness, and every tomorrow a vision of hope. Look well, therefore, to This Day -Sanskrit

Yesterday is but a memory, tomorrow is just a vision of hope, take action today

Yesterday is dead, forget it; tomorrow does not exist, don't worry; today is here, use it

Yesterday is gone; tomorrow never comes; today is here-get busy

Yesterday is history, tomorrow is a mystery, today is a gift, that's why we call it the present

Yesterday will not be called again -Slavic

*Yet let not each gay turn thy rapture move; for fools admire, but men of sense approve* –Pope

Yield to all and you will soon have nothing to yield -Aesop

Yielding is sometimes the best way of succeeding -Italian

Yin activity is centrifugal (dilating) and produces expansion, lightness, cold, etc. Yang activity is centripetal (constricting) and produces contraction, weight, heat, etc. Yin and yang together produce energy and all phenomena -1 of 12 theorems of the Unifying Principle, George

Ohsawa

Yin and yang are the two "activity poles" of the infinite pure expansion and are produced infinitely and continuously from the infinite pure expansion itself. One Infinity manifests itself into complementary and antagonistic tendencies, yin and yang, in its endless change -1 of 12 theorems of the Unifying Principle, George Ohsawa

Yin and yang, combined in an infinite variety of proportions, produce energy and all other visible and invisible phenomena. Yin and yang are manifested continuously from the eternal movement of One Infinite Universe -1 of 12 theorems of the Unifying Principle, George Ohsawa

Yin attracts yang; yang attracts yin -1 of 12 theorems of the Unifying Principle, George Ohsawa

Yin produces or becomes yang and yang produces or becomes yin at the extremes of development. Large yin attracts small yin. Large yang attracts small yang -1 of 12 theorems of the Unifying Principle, George Ohsawa

Yin repels yin; yang repels yang -1 of 12 theorems of the Unifying Principle, George Ohsawa

You a lady, I a lady, who is to put the sow out of doors?

You already possess everything necessary to become great -Crow

You always find something in the last place you look for it

You always have a choice, even if only of attitude

You are brave, intelligent, brilliant, attractive . . and gullible.

You are dust and you will become dust -Polish

You are mature when keeping a secret gives more satisfaction that telling it

You are much too intelligent to be affected by flattery

You are never fully dressed until you wear a smile

You are never given a wish without also being given the power to make it come true -Richard Bach

You are never justified in arguing -Hopi

You are not a fully fledged sailor unless you have sailed under full sail, and you have not built a wall unless you have rounded a corner -Irish

You are not fully dressed until you wear a smile

You are one person in the world, and you may also be the world to one person

You are only young once, but you can stay immature indefinitely

You are permitted in times of great danger to walk with the devil until you have crossed the bridge -Bulgarian

You are richer today if you have laughed, given or forgiven!

You are the greatest enemy if you are a coward, but if you are brave, you are your greatest friend

You are totally unique, just like everyone else

You are what you eat -German
You become like those you oppose
You become what you think about -Buddha
You can achieve almost anything by asking for help from others
You can always tell luck from ability by its duration
You can be a willing helper, but don't wait to be asked
You can be kind, or you can be correct
You can be rich, if not in possessions, in lack of want
You can buy a house, but not a home; a clock, but not time; a bed, but not sleep; a book, but not knowledge, a doctor's time, but not good health; position, but not respect, blood, but not life, and sex, but not love -Chinese
You can catch more flies with honey than vinegar- assuming you want to catch flies
You can discover more about a person in an hour of play than in a year of conversation -Plato
You can do anything with children if only you play with them -German
You can do more than strike while the iron is hot; you can make the iron hot by striking
You can drag a horse to water, but you can't make it drink
You can drive out nature with a pitchfork but she keeps on coming back -Horace
You can either control your temper, or let your temper control you
You can flatter more people into excelling than you can criticize out their apathy
You can fool people some of the time, but you can't fool them all of the time
You can fool some of the people all the time, and all of the people some of the time; but you can't fool all of the people all the time
You can fool too many of the people too much of the time -James Thurber
You can get many gentle sheep in a stable, but not when they are frightened
You can give a piece of advice, but not good luck along with that -Norwegian
You can harvest peaches and chestnuts in three years, and persimmons in eight years - Japanese
You can have no more of the fox than his skin -Danish
You can have too much of a good thing -Danish
You can judge a man by the company he keeps -Danish
You can lead a fool to wisdom, but you can't make him think
You can lead/take a horse to water but you can't make it drink -John Heywood
*You can make God laugh, for sure- tell him your plans for the future*

You can multiply happiness by dividing it with others
You can never enter the same river twice -Indian, Heraclitus
You can never exercise an open mind and an open moth at the same time
You can never plan the future by the past -Edmund Burke
You can often find in rivers what you cannot find in oceans -Indian
You can only be young once. But you can always be immature -Dave Barry
You can only die once -Portuguese
You can only lean against that which resists -Indian
You can outdistance that which is running after you, but not what is running inside you -Rwandan
You can pretend to be serious; you can't pretend to be witty -Sacha Guitry
You can save yourself a lot of trouble by not borrowing any
You can take a horse to the water, but you can't make him drink
You can take the boy out of the country but you can't take the country out of the boy -Rwandan
You can take the day off, but you can never put it back
You can take the man out of the country, but you can't take the country out of a man
You can tell how big a person is by what it takes to discourage him
You can throw a cat however you want, it always stays on its feet -Polish
You can't act like a skunk without someone getting wind of it
You can't antagonize and influence at the same time
You can't be a true winner until you have lost
You can't any more give away something you don't have than you can come back from a place you haven't been to
You can't catch the wind in a net
You can't depend on your eyes when your imagination is out of focus -Mark Twain
You can't eat your cake and have it too
You can't expect perfection every time
You can't get ahead if you are concentrating on getting even
You can't get blood/milk from a stone
You can't get rich if you look after your relatives properly -Navajo
You can't grow hair on a billiard ball
You can't have too many friends, or too few enemies
You can't hold onto the side of the boat and swim to shore at the same time
You can't make a silk purse out of a sow's ear
You can't make an omelet without breaking eggs
You can't put old heads on young shoulders
You can't put out a fire with oil

You can't put thanks in your pocket
You can't see life, ya know. It's a man you see movin' you call life -Rastafarian, Jamaica
You can't see wisdom, but you can see its reflection. Its reflection is happiness, fearlessness, and kindness -Sylvia Boorstein
You can't sell the cow and keep the milk
You can't spoil a good thing
You can't squeeze blood from a turnip
You can't steal second base and keep one foot on first -Frederick B. Wilson
You can't take it with you, but you can send it on ahead -Rev. Eikenroetter
You can't tell the depth of the well by the length of the handle on its pump
You can't tell which way the train went by looking at its tracks
You cannot both want the horse to be the best, and also want the horse not to eat any hay -Chinese
You cannot break through a wall with [only] your forehead -Russian
You cannot build a house for last year's summer -Ethiopian
You cannot build a reputation on the things you are going to do
You cannot burn the candle at both ends
You cannot carry water in a sieve -Russian
You cannot carve rotten wood -Chinese
You cannot catch a flea with gloves -Albanian
You cannot catch an old bird by offering it chaff -Russian
You cannot catch old birds with chaff
You cannot clap with one hand
You cannot compare the living with the dead -Nigerian
You cannot damage a wrecked whip -Italian
You cannot depend on your eyes when your imagination is out of focus -Mark Twain
You cannot discover new oceans unless you have the courage to lose sight of the shore -Italian
You cannot do a kindness too soon, for you never know how soon it will be too late -Ralph Waldo Emerson
You cannot draw blood from a turnip -Italian
You cannot dream yourself into a character; you must hammer and forge yourself one -James A. Froude
You cannot drink and whistle at the same time -Danish
You cannot eat your cake and have your cake -Cervantes
You cannot expect a person to see eye to eye with you when you're looking down on him
You cannot flay the same ox twice
You cannot get oil out of a wall -French

You cannot get to the top by sitting on your bottom
Who gossips to you will gossip about you - Turkish
You cannot have peace longer than your neighbour chooses -Danish
You cannot have two forenoons in the same day
You cannot have your cake and eat it -Danish
You cannot hunt with a tied dog -Albanian
You cannot judge a tree by its bark
You cannot lose what you never had
You cannot make a crab walk straight
You cannot make a good archbishop out of a rogue -Danish
You cannot make a good hunting-horn of a pig's tail -Danish
You cannot make a hawk of a buzzard -French
You cannot make a silk purse out of a sow's ear -Irish
You cannot make an ass drink if he is not thirsty -French
You cannot make an omelet without breaking eggs -French
You cannot make bricks without straw -French
You cannot pull a fish out of a pond without labour -Russian
You cannot pull hard with a broken rope -Danish
You cannot push anyone up the ladder, unless he is willing to climb himself
You cannot put an old head on young shoulders
You cannot put old heads on young shoulders
You cannot reason with a hungry belly; it has no ears -Greek
You cannot ride two horses with one ass -Russian
You cannot roast corn with two eyes -Nigerian
You cannot run with the hare and hunt with the hounds -Nigerian
You cannot sail as you would, but as the wind blows -Danish
You cannot see the city for the houses
You cannot see the spark in flint, or the soul in man
You cannot sell the cow and sup the milk
You cannot serve God and mammon -Danish, Biblical
You cannot shake hands with a clenched fist -Indira Ghandi
You cannot share any experience with another. You can only share with others what you experience for yourself and allow others to share with you what they experience for themselves.
You cannot shear the sheep closer than the skin -Danish
You cannot shift an old tree without it dying -Danish
You cannot sit on the road to success for if you do, you will get run over
You cannot take a cow from a man who has none -Danish
You cannot take a shirt from a naked man -Danish
You cannot tickle a hungry person – Masai
You cannot unsay a cruel word -Country wisdom
You cannot unscramble eggs -North American

You cannot write in the chimney with charcoal -Russian
You can't be truly rude until you understand good manners -Rita Mae Brown
You can't beat a dead horse - Richard Trench
You can't build a relationship with a hammer
You can't buy an inch of time with an inch of gold -Chinese
You can't buy fate -Ferengi Rule of Acquisition
You can't buy heaven with money -Maltese
You can't buy love
You can't chop down a forest without splinters flying -Russian
You can't control the wind, but you can adjust your sails
You can't damage a smile by cracking it
You can't do much about the length of your life, but you can do a lot about its depth and width
You can't eat your cake and have it too -John Heywood
You can't expect people to see eye to eye with you if you look down on them
You can't fit a square peg in a round hole
You can't free a fish from water -Ferengi Rule of Acquisition
You can't get at the precious sago without first breaking the bark -Malay
You can't get blood out of a stone -English
You can't get blood out of a turnip -English
You can't hatch chickens from fried eggs -Dutch
You can't have it both ways
You can't have peace any longer than your neighbor pleases - Dutch
You can't hold a man down unless you stay down with him
You can't judge a horse by its harness -Thomas Fuller
You can't keep a chip on the shoulder you put to the wheel
You can't lock down either wind or woman -Japanese
You can't make a deal if you're dead -Ferengi Rule of Acquisition
You can't make a fact out of an opinion by raising your voice
You can't make a good shaft of a pig's tail -Portuguese
You can't make a silk purse out of a sow's ear -Portuguese
You can't pick up two melons with one hand -Persian
You can't play all the time - Aesop
You can't please everyone -Persian
You can't polish a turd -Persian
You can't push on a rope -Persian
You can't put new wine in old bottles -Persian
You can't see the whole sky through a bamboo tube -Japanese
You can't separate peace from freedom because no one can be at peace unless he has his freedom –Malcolm X
You can't sew buttons on your neighbor's mouth -Russian

You can't solve a problem with the same kind of thinking that created it
-Albert Einstein
You can't squeeze blood from a rock -Persian
You can't steal second base and keep your foot on first
You can't stop a pig from wallowing in the mud -Yoruba
You can't take blood from a stone -Persian
You can't take it with you, but you can send it on ahead!  -Reverend Ike
You can't talk to a judge empty-handed -Russian
You can't teach an old dog new tricks
You can't tell a book by its cover - American
You can't unsay a cruel thing
You can't use your friends and have them too
You can't wake a person who is pretending to be asleep -Navajo
You can't win a fight without attacking
You can't win them all
You carry heaven and hell with you
You catch more flies with honey than you do with vinegar -Ben Franklin
You come with a cat and call it a rabbit -Cameroonian
You could drive a stick man crazy
You create your own reality
You cried for night. It falls. Now cry in darkness.
You do not need a whip to urge on an obedient horse -Russian
You do not need to leave your room. Remain sitting at your table and
listen. Do not even listen, simply wait. Do not even wait, be still and
solitary. The world will freely offer itself to you  to be unmasked, it has no
choice. It will roll in ecstasy at your feet -Frantz Kafka
You do not need to vanquish your enemies.  Wake up to the fact that you
have no enemies.
You do not really understand something unless you can explain it to your
grandmother -Russian
You don't get what you don't ask for
You don't drown by falling in the water; you drown by staying there -Edwin
Louis Cole
You don't get anywhere unless you try
You don't get something for nothing -Russian
You don't grow rich by a big income, but by small expenses
You don't have to put out the fire when all is burnt out –Norwegian
You don't know what you've got until it's gone
You don't know where your shadow will fall
You don't need to furnish references to borrow trouble
You don't reap grapes from thistles -Arabic
You don't show a fool a job half done -Hebrew
You don't stop laughing because you grow old. You grow old because

you stop laughing.
You either want to do a thing or your don't. It's seldom that you can't.
You enjoy fruit from what your ancestors planted -Japanese
You get a body at birth –Rule 1 of 10 Life Rules
You get what you earn/deserve
You get what you pay for, and pay for what you get
You have a lifetime to work, but children are only young once -Polish
You have achieved success if you have lived well, laughed often and loved much -Emerson
You have determination only if you finish every job you start
You have hit the nail on the head
You have lent and not recovered; and if recovered, not so much; and if so much, not such; and if such, a mortal enemy -Portuguese
You have many strings to your bow -Portuguese
You have married a beauty? So much the worse for you -Italian
You have no goats, and yet you sell kids
You have nobody to blame but yourself if you stumble more than once over the same stump -Italian
You have poise if you can be ill at ease inconspicuously
You have to crawl before you can walk
You have to earn respect
You have to kiss a lot of toads before you find a handsome prince -North American
You have to take the bitter with the sweet
You have to wonder about humans, they think God is dead and Elvis is alive!
You know the lion from its claw -Latin
You learn from your mistakes -German
You live with wolves, you howl like a wolf -Russian
You look for the horse you ride on -Russian
You made your bed, now you must lie in it
You made your own bed, now lie in it -German
You make the failure complete when you stop trying
You make the road by walking on it -Nicaraguan
You make your own happiness -German
You may always find an opportunity in your sleeve, if you like -Danish
You may as well be hung for a sheep as a lamb -Danish
You may as well expect pears from an elm -Cervantes
You may as well give a good beating as a bad one -French
You may be deceived if you trust to much, but you will live in torment if you don't trust enough -Frank Crane
You may bend the sapling, but not the tree
You may call that your own which no one can take from you -Danish

You may cook in small pots aw well as in large ones -Danish
You may delay, but time will not -Ben Franklin
You may force a horse to the water, but you cannot make him drink -Danish
You may force a man to shut his eyes, but not to sleep -Danish
You may force an ox to the water, but you cannot make him drink -Danish
You may gain by fair words what may fail you by angry ones -Danish
*You may get something off a bone, but nothing off a stone* -Danish
You may go farther and fare worse
You may keep yourself safe from fire, but not from a bad man -Portuguese
You may know by a handful the whole sack
You may know the horse by his harness
You may know the lion by his claw -French
You may laugh at a friend's roof; don't laugh at his sleeping accommodation -Kenyan
You may light another's candle at your own without loss -Danish
You may live it up occasionally, but then you'll have to live it down
You may not be able to keep trouble from visiting you, but you don't have to let it sit down and stay -Country wisdom
You may not know how the turtle got into the tree, but you can be sure it had help
You may not win, but you might make the one ahead of you break the record
You may often feel that heavily on your back which you took lightly on your conscience -Danish
You may preach ever so long to the wolf, he will nevertheless call for the lamb before night -Danish
You may run short of lemon juice for rubbing, but never will copper turn to gold -Swahili
You may shut your doors against a thief, but not against a liar -Danish
You may speak with your gold and make other tongues silent -Danish
You may take a horse to the water, but you can't make him drink -Danish
You miss 100% of the shots you don't take -Wayne Gretzky
You must ask your neighbour if you shall live in peace
You must be strong to pull a rope against a stronger -Danish
*You must believe to achieve*
You must contrive to bake with the flour you have -Danish
You must crack the nuts before eating the kernel -Irish
You must crawl before you can walk
You must cut your coat according to your cloth -Irish
You must empty a box before you fill it again -Irish
You must grease the wheels if you would have the cart run -Italian

You must have good luck to catch hares with a drum -Danish
You must howl with the wolves when you are among them -Danish
You must judge a maiden at the kneading trough, and not in a dance -Danish
You must kill the spider to get rid of the cobweb -Maltese
You must knock a long while against an alder-bush before you get a swarm of bees out of it -Danish
You must live with a person to know a person. If you want to know me, come and live with me -Irish
You must live your life from beginning to end- no-one else can do it for you –Hopi
You must lose a fly to catch a trout -George Herbert
You must neither strive for truth nor seek to lose your illusions -The Shodoka
You must not pledge your own health
You must not throw stones into your neighbor's garden -French
You must reap what you have sown
You must shift your sail with the wind -Italian
You must take the fat with the lean -Italian
You must walk a long while behind a wild goose before you find an ostrich feather -Danish
You need a sharp ax for a tough bough -Russian
You need not find a shelter for an old ox -Portuguese
*You needn't be afraid of a barking dog, but you should be afraid of a silent dog*
You never fail until you stop trying
You never get change from a priest, or remnants from a tailor -Russian
You never know a man until you've eaten a whole sack of salt together -Russian
You never know how a cow catches a rabbit -Dutch
You never know the length of a snake until it is dead
You never know until you find out
You never know what is enough unless you know what is more than enough -William Blake
You never know what lies right around the corner
You never know what you can do till you try -Dutch
You never know what you've got till it's gone
*You never know when someone May catch a dream from you- You never know when a little word Or something you may do- May open the windows Of a mind that seeks the light- The way you live may not matter at all, But you never know, it might*
You never know your luck
You never miss a slice from a cut loaf -English

You never miss the water till the well runs dry -English
You never really know your friends from your enemies until the ice breaks -Eskimo
You never test the depth of a river with both feet
You often meet your fate on the road you take to avoid it -French
You only have power over people as long as you don't take everything away from them. But when you've robbed a person of everything he's no longer in your power- he's free again - Alexander Solzhenitsyn
You only know what you do -Lester Levenson
You pays your money and you takes your choice -French
You play with edged tools -French
You probably won't find a good stallion in the mule line
You roll my log and I'll roll yours
You scratch my back and I'll scratch yours
You serve life so much better when you live from choice, not default
You should water your children like you water a tree -Hopi
You should, like a candle, burn yourself out to give light to others
*You snooze, you lose*
You tell by the work, not by the clothes -Albanian
You think education is expensive? Try ignorance
You think you are strong like the corn plant, yet the bean vine is already choking you -Madagasy
You want it bad, you'll get it bad
You will always have plenty of money if you let the rest of the world go buy
You will be presented with lessons throughout life –Rule 2 of 10 Life Rules
You will be troubled with what you have no knowledge of , if you seek out the affairs of another -Swahili
You will break the bow if you keep it always bent -Greek
You will catch more flies with a spoonful of honey than with a gallon of vinegar -Slavic
You will forget all the rules at birth –Rule 10 of 10 Life Rules
You will go out on a limb, because that's where the fruit grows
You will go safest in the middle -Latin
You will hate a beautiful song if you sing it often -Korean
You will never find time for anything. If you want time you must make it -Charles Buxton
You will never get indigestion from swallowing your pride
You will not be loved if you think of yourself alone -Italian
You will not dare mistreat the face you see in the morning -Palestinian
You will not get a big job done from whom does not want a small one -Albanian

You will not see many with green eyes -Portuguese
You will probably be happy in the same degree as you are helpful to others
You will sleep as you make your bed -Slavic
You win some, you lose some
You won't get what you don't ask for
You won't even get started if you wait for all the conditions to be "just right"
*You work for Coca Cola, you drink  Coca Cola  [And the dentist gets your moola]*
You work for Coca Cola, you don't drink Pepsi
You'll never get ahead of anybody you're tryin' to get even with -Country wisdom
You'd better wise up
You'll get along with the boss if he goes his way and you go his
You'll never do anything behind you that won't come up in front of you
You'll never plow a field by turning it over in your mind -Irish
You'll notice that a turtle only makes progress when it sticks out its neck
*Young cats will mouse, young apes will louse* -Dutch
Young dogs have sharp teeth -Danish
*Young folk, silly folk; old folk, cold folk* -Dutch
Young folks think old folks to be fools, but old folks know young folks to be fools -Dutch
Young fools think that the old are dotards, but the old have forgotten more than the young fools know -Dutch
Young man may die, but old men must [die]
Young men may die, old men must -English
Young men's knocks, old men feel -English
Young people don't know what age is, and old people forget what youth was -English
Young people must be taught, old ones be honoured -Danish
Young people tell what they are doing, old people what they have done, and fools what they wish to do -French
Young pigs grunt as old pigs grunted before them -Danish
Young saint, old devil; young whore, old saint
Young twigs may be bent, but not old trees -Dutch
Young wood makes a hot fire -Greek
Your answers lie inside of you —Rule 9 of 10 Life Rules
Your best friend is yourself
Your close neighbor is better than your faraway brother -Arab
Your conscience may not keep you from doing wrong, but it sure keeps you from enjoying it
Your conscience, like a buzzing bee, can make you feel uneasy without

stinging you
Your dreams come true when you act to turn them into realities
Your enemy makes you wiser -Italian
Your eyes eat images the way your mouth eats food, and you become what you eat -Native American
Your fences need to be horse-high, pig-tight and bull-strong -Country wisdom
Your friend has a friend; don't tell him -Jewish
Your friend lends and your enemy asks payment -Dutch
Your good fortune sometimes makes false friends; poor fortune points them out
Your health comes first; you can always hang yourself later -Yiddish
Your heart understands what your head cannot yet conceive; trust your heart
Your knowledge is nothing when no one else knows that you know it -Latin
Your neighbor's apples are the sweetest -Yiddish
Your own rags are better than another's gown -Hausa
Your skills pave the road for you -Japanese
Your son is your son until he marries, but your daughter is your daughter until you die -Irish
Your soul to God, your body to dust, your property to your relatives, and the waves caress the sands on the beach
Your soul to God, your body to dust, your property to your relatives, because thus it has been found written -Maltese
Your success and happiness lie in you...resolve to keep happy and your joy and you shall form an invincible host against difficulties -Helen Keller
*Your thoughts are like the sculptor's blows, each the inner spirit shows*
Your time is the greatest gift you can give to someone
Your wife and sheep, early at home -Portuguese
Your windmill dwindles into a nutcrack -Portuguese
Your words can come back to haunt you -German
You're only young once. After that you need another excuse for doing childish things.
Youth does not mind where it sets its foot -Irish
Youth has a small head -Irish
Youth is a blunder; manhood a struggle, old age a regret
Youth is life's seedtime
Youth is such a wonderful thing; it's a shame to waste it on children
Youth is the season of hope, enterprise, and energy, to a nation as well as an individual
Youth is wasted on the young -Irish
Youth lives on hope, old age on remembrance -French

*Youth looks forward, and age, backward*
Youth may stray afar yet return at last -French
Youth must be served -French
Youth must have its fling -French
Youth sheds many a skin –Irish
Youth will have its course
You've got to do your own growing, no matter how tall your grandfather was -Irish
You've got to stare the cat down out of the tree -Dutch
*Zeal is blind when it encroaches on the rights of others*
Zeal without knowledge is a runaway horse
Zeal without knowledge is like fire without light -English
Zeal without knowledge is the sister of folly -English
Zeal, not ability, is the father of success
Zen is a way of liberation, concerned not with discovering what is good or bad or advantageous, but what is -Alan Watts
Zen is not some kind of excitement, but merely concentration on our usual everyday routine -Shunkyu Suzuki
Zen is selling water by the river -Zen
Zen master: Who binds you? The seeker of liberty: No one binds me
Zen master: Then why seek liberation?  -Zen


The search for light and truth is never ending.


What proverbs have guided your life?

www.ingramcontent.com/pod-product-compliance
Lightning Source LLC
Chambersburg PA
CBHW060256290526
45789CB00001B/335